COMPANY B

6TH MICHIGAN CAVALRY

COMPANY B
6TH MICHIGAN CAVALRY
THIRD EDITION

Copyright© 2012 by Mark S. Stowe
1st Edition – June 2002
2nd Edition – July 2002

ISBN: 1439286434
ISBN-13: 9781439286432

Library of Congress Control Number: 2012903790
CreateSpace, North Charleston, South Carolina

COMPANY B

6TH MICHIGAN CAVALRY

Mark S. Stowe

DEDICATION

THIS WORK WAS WRITTEN IN HONOR
OF THE MEN OF COMPANY B
6TH MICHIGAN VOLUNTEER CAVALRY REGIMENT
MICHIGAN CAVALRY BRIGADE

AND DEDICATED TO
THE MEN OF COMPANY D
1ST BATTALION
503RD PARACHUTE INFANTRY REGIMENT
173RD AIRBORNE BRIGADE

FOR OUR
BAND OF BROTHERS

KENT (DOG-MAN)

BRENT (GOOSE)

AL (TENNESSEE)

DAVE

J.Q. (THE Q)

JIMMY

TONY

&

C. C.

CONTENTS

DEDICATION v
FOR OUR BAND OF BROTHERS vii
ACKNOWLEDGEMENTS xi
FOREWORD xv
GRAND RAPIDS – CAMP KELLOGG 1
WASHINGTON, D.C. – GUARDING THE CAPITAL . . 17
GETTYSBURG – FIRST CAMPAIGN 29
PURSUIT – PUSHING BACK TO VIRGINIA 45
GETTYSBURG'S AFTERMATH 61
WINTER IN VIRGINIA 69
ACROSS THE RAPIDAN 83
THE SHENANDOAH VALLEY 99
APPOMATTOX AND THE GRAND REVIEW 111
ON THE GREAT PLAINS 119
AFTER THE WAR 141
APPENDIX A 155
APPENDIX B 159
APPENDIX C 163
APPENDIX D 167
BIBLIOGRAPHY 177
INDEX OF PERSONS 181

ACKNOWLEDGEMENTS

M any people helped in gathering the information for this work. I was very fortunate to find several descendants of soldiers in Company B who also have a love of history. They shared their ancestor's letters, diaries, notebooks, artifacts, and especially their friendship with me and my wife, and we are very grateful to them.

GARRY BUSH – Descendant of Daniel and Henry Washington (Wash) Stewart. Garry currently lives in California and is an officer in the U.S. Marine Corps Reserve. Garry wrote a very good article on the fight at Falling Waters for Gettysburg magazine.

DAVID VANDYKE – Descendant of Daniel H. Powers. The material he and his parents made available had a very valuable impact on this history. David lives in Indiana and pursues his interest in history.

ELOISE HAVEN – Descendant of Allen D. Pease. Eloise is retired and living in Michigan. She is a former Air Force officer, and holds a Masters Degree in history from Central Michigan University. Eloise has written several books, of history and historical fiction, and has made many contributions to libraries and organizations on the local and national level.

RICHARD AND RUTH ANN HAMILTON – Richard is a descendant of George T. Patten. He and Ruth Ann are retired and live in Arizona. Richard holds a Masters Degree in Industrial Supervision from Western Michigan University. While dressed in a uniform and assuming the role of his Civil

War ancestor, he and Ruth Ann, also in period dress, give presentations to libraries, historical societies, and other interested organizations. Richard has written several books on various subjects, one of which is about his ancestor. He and Ruth Ann have become good friends.

Thank you all very much! Without your help and encouragement, this work would not exist.

We were honored as well to have the support of some very fine historians and professionals who help preserve our heritage.

JOHN T. KREPPS is a Licensed Battlefield Guide at Gettysburg National Military Park. He wrote a well researched book entitled "A Strong and Sudden Onslaught: The Cavalry Action at Hanover, Pennsylvania," which covered the fights on June 30, 1863. John took us on a detailed tour of the area in which Company B was fighting that day. It was a thoroughly enjoyable afternoon, and very much appreciated.

BARBARA MADISON, Genealogist, Historian, Teacher, and Friend.

TED ALEXANDER, Historian at Antietam National Battlefield Park, and CURT GALL, Park Ranger of the Chesapeake and Ohio Canal National Historical Park at Williamsport, Maryland. Each year they hold a weekend long study of the Confederate retreat from Gettysburg, including a very pleasant five-mile walk along the Potomac, which helped us understand the campaign much better.

GEORGE FRANKS, Part-owner of the Donnelly House and property along Falling Waters Road, where the charge of Companies B and F fell on Archer's Brigade. George also wrote an excellent article on the fight there for Strategy and Tactics Magazine.

GERALD HARLOW, President of the Trevilian Station Battlefield Foundation, in Louisa County, Virginia. Gerald took us on a very enjoyable tour of the battlefield, outlining

ACKNOWLEDGEMENTS

details of the action, and preservation challenges faced by his organization.

TRISH POPOVITCH, former Historian and Curator of the Deer Creek Museum at Glenrock, Wyoming. She provided important materials and information about Company B's duty station in the summer of 1865.

DON HARVEY, author of "Michigan in the War" website.

A special note of thanks goes to KAROLEE GILLMAN, of the Grand Rapids History and Special Collections Department at the Grand Rapids Public Library. My wife and I appreciate her help, encouragement, and friendship. Our library is a better place to conduct research and work because she is there. Thank you Karolee.

Our appreciation goes to the staffs of Archives, Libraries, Historical Sites, and Organizations which aided in this work.

Grand Rapids History and Special Collections Department, Grand Rapids Public Library, Grand Rapids, Michigan

Hekman Library, Calvin College, Grand Rapids, Michigan

Regional History Collections, Western Michigan University, Kalamazoo, Michigan

Bentley Historical Library, University of Michigan, Ann Arbor, Michigan

Burton Historical Collection, Detroit Public Library, Detroit, Michigan

State Archives of Michigan, Library of Michigan, Lansing, Michigan

National Archives, Washington, D.C.

Library of Congress, Washington, D.C.

Gettysburg National Military Park, Gettysburg, Pennsylvania

Antietam National Battlefield and Cemetery, Sharpsburg, Maryland

Chesapeake and Ohio Canal National Park, at Williamsport, Maryland

Army Heritage and Education Center, Carlisle Pennsylvania
Trevilian Station Battlefield Foundation, Trevilian, Virginia
Petersburg National Battlefield, Petersburg, Virginia
Oregon National Historic Trail, in Kansas, Nebraska, and Wyoming
Fort Kearny State Historic Site, Kearny, Nebraska
Fort Laramie National Historic Site, Fort Laramie, Wyoming
Deer Creek Museum, and Glenrock Historical Commission, Glenrock, Wyoming
Fort Caspar Museum, Casper, Wyoming
Johnson County Visitors Bureau, Buffalo, Wyoming
Little Bighorn Battlefield National Monument, Crow Agency, Montana

Special thanks go to my son and daughter-in-law, CHRIS and KELLY (SMALLWOOD) STOWE for their inspiration and support, and to my son JEFF STOWE and his fiancee BRITTANY BILSKI for their encouragement and technical support. Brittany was a big help in guiding us through the use of hardware and software.

Finally, and most important, is the support I have from my wife, UTE (ZIEGNER) STOWE. Born in East Germany and raised in West Berlin, she is no stranger to hardship, pain, and danger. She refused to allow it to change or embitter her. Her strength and positivity are infectious, and I am very fortunate to have her love, loyalty, and friendship. More than anything else, her strength, faith, and encouragement keep me going. Thank you sweetheart – I love you too.

FOREWORD

While growing up in Michigan, I developed a strong interest in military history. During that time, the Centennial of the Civil War and the Sesquicentennial of the War of 1812 were observed. American heritage was popular then, and I was happily caught up in it. My Dad told me about my Great-Grandfather, who had fought and died in the Civil War, and that my middle name had been given to me in honor of him. No one knew any more than that.

Later, after many years of military service and overseas assignments, including an extended combat tour, my perspectives had changed, but not my interest in the subject. Taking up the study of history, and focusing on military history, I discovered my Great-Grandfather had been in the Michigan Cavalry Brigade commanded by Brigadier General George A. Custer. I began to collect the information presented in this work. In many ways, Company B is very much like other cavalry organizations of the period, but it also had experiences that made it stand out.

Not long ago, I became a member of the Army Heritage Center Foundation, which supports the Army Heritage and Education Center at Carlisle, Pennsylvania. Their motto – "Telling the Army story…one soldier at a time," helped inspire me to do this third edition of Company B, 6th Michigan Cavalry, in observance of the Sesquicentennial of the Civil War.

Errors from the second edition have been corrected and some new information has been added. Any further errors or omissions are, of course, mine alone. Although I am extremely pleased to tell their story, and very proud my Great-Grandfather was one of them, I am cognizant this is a rough-done and personal project. This story is about citizen soldiers. All but one of the commanders of Company B had been enlisted men and non-commissioned officers before being promoted to command.

I humbly present this short, modest history of a group of ordinary young men who sometimes did extraordinary things in the performance of their duty, and I am dedicating it to another group of young men it was my privilege and honor to serve with. This is the story of soldiers who, like all soldiers throughout time, and for whatever reasons, risked everything for what they perceived as a better tomorrow.

GRAND RAPIDS –
CAMP KELLOGG

Francis W. Kellogg, honorable representative from the Fourth Congressional District in Michigan, was a very busy man in the summer of 1862. The American Civil War had entered its second year, and the United States was failing in its effort to subdue its rebellious southern brethren. On July 2, President Lincoln issued a call for 300,000 more volunteers. In response, the lumberman-turned-politician sought and obtained permission directly from the Secretary of War, Edwin M. Stanton, with the approval of Governor Austin Blair, to raise two regiments of volunteer cavalry. Kellogg was familiar with the process, as he had raised the Second and Third Regiments of Michigan Cavalry the previous year. In August, he began organizing what would become the Sixth regiment, and served for a time as its nominal Colonel.[1]

Congress had established the organization of volunteer cavalry regiments in 1861. On July 17, 1862, the table of organization was amended slightly, retaining its basic composition of twelve companies - or troops as they could now be called - but authorizing an increase from 104 to 112 men for each. Recruiting commenced immediately. Men of good standing in their communities were offered commissions in the regiment if they recruited a minimum of seventy-eight men by the rendezvous date. They had little trouble accomplishing

1

the task. Recent Confederate success on the battlefield, with their forces ranging north into Maryland and Kentucky, compelled many men to enlist. Patriotic meetings were held in local schools where recruiters gave speeches to persuade men to join their companies. In some instances, they worked the same communities, and there was some intense but friendly competition. Prospective officers who recruited Company B were Warren Comstock and Charles Bolza of Grand Rapids, and Charles Storrs of Blendon Township in Ottawa County. [2]

Rendezvous for the regiment was set for Saturday, September 13, 1862 in Grand Rapids. In some cases, as for James H. Kidd of Ionia, the date was extended a few days. Men arrived by train, stagecoach, wagon, horseback, and on foot. They were organized into companies according to their recruitment, and set up in a temporary camp by the Grand River. Close to a thousand men were gathered to form the regiment, and nearly ninety of them belonged to the company to be designated with the letter B. Most of them were farmers or tradesmen from communities in Kent or adjacent counties. There were contingents from Big Rapids and Newaygo in the north, and even from Livingston County and elsewhere in eastern Michigan, who had been enlisted originally for the Fifth Michigan, but the majority came from Grand Rapids or the small towns and villages nearby. [3]

Young farmers and farm laborers like Harvey Smith of Wyoming, Oscar Stout of Courtland Township, and Henry Welch of Gaines Township came to town for the rendezvous. Walter Waite, a neighbor of Charles Storrs, traveled in from Blendon. Allen Pease maintained a home in Nunica in Ottawa County, but worked in Grand Rapids. Tradesmen like Stephen Stowe, Edwin Whitney and his brother William, arrived by the plank road from Wayland in Allegan County. Forty-eight year old Daniel Stewart and his seventeen year old son, Henry

Washington Stewart, or "Wash" as he was called, left their farm in Wyoming to join the cavalry.[4]

On Monday, September 15, a confident and trim looking young officer reported for duty as commander of Company B. James Kidd described him. "With a brisk step and a military air a young man of about my own age entered (Headquarters), whose appearance and manner were prepossessing. He looked younger than his years, was not large but had a well-knit, compact frame of medium height. He was alert in look and movement, his face ruddy with health, his eyes bright and piercing, his head crowned with a thick growth of brown hair cut rather short...and appeared every inch the soldier." His name was Peter A. Weber, and he was twenty-one years old.[5]

Weber had been a librarian for the Grand Rapids Library Association and a store clerk before the war. He lived in town with his widowed mother and two sisters. In June 1861, he joined the Third Michigan Infantry, made Corporal, and was at Blackburn's Ford during the first battle of Bull Run. In September of that year, he was commissioned a Lieutenant and Battalion Adjutant in the Second Michigan Cavalry, which was sent to the western army commanded by Major General John Pope. He was detached to his Brigade Staff, and later, Division Staff in the spring of 1862, which provided him with some command experience. The congressional act that changed the structure of volunteer cavalry units also eliminated his position as a Battalion Adjutant. Learning of the formation of new regiments in Michigan, Weber left federal service on August 31, 1862 and returned to Michigan, where he was a recruiting officer in the Kalamazoo district for a few days before reporting to "Colonel" Kellogg in Grand Rapids as a Captain and Company Commander.[6]

PETER A. WEBER
FIRST COMMANDER OF COMPANY B

Photo Courtesy of the Burton Historical Collection, Detroit Public Library

The Fifth Michigan Cavalry, organized at Detroit, had an over-filled, additional or supernumerary company, made up of men primarily from western Michigan. Sent to Grand Rapids as a nucleus for the Sixth, it became Company A. Captain Weber, because of his experience, would command Company B, which included the extra men from Company A. All remaining companies had to compete for their designations, from C through M, based on their proficiency in drill.[7]

As a guide to becoming horse soldiers, the Sixth Cavalry used a relatively new manual for training. Philip St. George Cooke, a dragoon of the old army and a Brigadier General of Cavalry, wrote the book. Cooke was a Virginian with sons in the Confederate Army, and his son-in-law was the Confederate cavalry leader J.E.B. Stuart, who would oppose the Sixth Michigan in many of its battles. Adopted for use by the U.S. Army in 1861 and published the following year, the manual emphasized operating on horseback and in single ranks, rather than the old way of using the horses for transportation and fighting primarily on foot in two ranks. Illustrated text described a system of training for horses and men. Individual troopers were trained within squads of eight or nine men – at first dismounted, then progressing to horseback. When a prescribed level of proficiency was reached, the training included larger bodies of troops called platoons, which consisted of two squads. Beyond that was company drill. Companies consisted of four platoons. Squads were led by Corporals, platoons by Sergeants and/or Lieutenants, and Captain Weber commanded the company.[8]

Soldiering was unfamiliar to virtually everyone in Company B, with the notable exception of Weber. New officers and non-commissioned officers had to work hard to stay one step ahead of the men they were training. Camp life, like most military service, was a strange mixture of intense activity and extreme boredom, while those in charge learned what they needed to do. One of their first acts was to change the location of the camp. Low ground by the river was too soggy for a large body of men to live and train, especially after recent rains. On Friday after Rendezvous, the camp was moved up the ridge to the end of Lyon Street, and named Camp Kellogg, in honor of the regiment's patron. Regimental equipment didn't include enough tents for everyone, so officers lived in wall tents, and crude wooden barracks were constructed for the troopers.[9]

Non-commissioned officers, Corporals and Sergeants, helped Officers control and train the men. Most of these men were officially promoted to their ranks when the regiment was mustered in, based on evaluations made by Captain Weber. Some took their leadership roles on at the beginning because of known ability or special qualifications. First Sergeant, or Orderly Sergeant, was Daniel Powers of Grand Rapids. Powers, a competent and well-read young man, had been a store clerk prior to joining the army. Quartermaster Sergeant was George T. Patten of Alpine Township. Patten, a serious and very capable man, had farmed with his father prior to enlisting. He left a wife and two-year-old son to do what he felt was a solemn duty. His cousin, Charles H. Patten of Grand Rapids was the Regimental Quartermaster, so his appointment as Quartermaster Sergeant for the company had its advantages. Pliny Smith of Grand Rapids was the Commissary Sergeant. Troop Sergeants were Egbert Conklin of Alpine, William Keyes of Jamestown Township in Ottawa County, Nelson Thomas from Brighton in Livingston County, and Edwin Robinson and Edmund Dikeman of Grand Rapids. Corporals were James Johnson and Harvey Potter of Alpine, James Keater of Grand Rapids, David McVean of Lowell, John Maxfield and Dorr Skeels of Ottawa County, Orson Odell of Plainfield, and John Platt of Brighton. This was the original command structure of Company B. As time went on, it would undergo constant and sometimes sweeping change.[10]

Regimental Order #1 was issued soon after camp was established, which set a daily schedule for training. It was adjusted slightly in Order #3 and posted. It looked like this.

Reveille and Roll Call	5am
Drill	5:30
Recall	6:30
Breakfast	6:40

Fatigue	8 am
Recall & Guard Mount	8:30
Drill	9am
(Officers drilled separately during these morning sessions)	
Recall	11am
Orders	11:05
Dinner Roll Call	11:30
Drill	2pm
Recall	4pm
Retreat Roll Call	Sunset
Tatoo	8:30
Taps	9pm

Slowly yet steadily, B Company made progress. Camp was shaping up and uniforms were issued, which consisted of knee high cavalry boots, reinforced trousers, shell jackets, and forage caps. Horses, some of the best that could be found in Michigan, as well as the necessary equipment, also arrived. Shelters were built for them in camp. Men were drilled as much as possible despite not having to compete. Captain Weber's knowledge and experience helped immeasurably in preparing the company for war.[11]

Thirty-nine year old George Gray, an attorney in Grand Rapids, was named "Lieutenant-Colonel Commanding," and took charge of the regiment and the camp. Even though the other officers believed the position of Colonel, and command of the regiment, should go to an experienced regular army officer, a petition was passed around to appoint Gray to the position, which they all signed and sent to Governor Blair. At about this time, Blair gave command of the Sixth to twenty-two year old William Mann, Lieutenant-Colonel of the Fifth Michigan Cavalry, then at Detroit. Next day a delegation from Grand Rapids, headed by Congressman Kellogg and Gray's old law partner, Judge Solomon Withey, hurried to Detroit to meet with Blair. They convinced Mann to take command of the Seventh Michigan Cavalry, which was Kellogg's other regiment also forming in Grand Rapids. This enabled Blair to reverse his decision, and name Gray as Colonel and commander of the Sixth.[12]

Assisting Colonel Gray were three Majors commanding Battalions within the Regiment made up of four companies each. Regimental Orders 12 and 13 established them.

First Battalion consisted of Companies A, D, F, & I under Major Thaddeus Foote.

Second Battalion consisted of Companies B, E, G, & K under Major Elijah Waters.

Third Battalion consisted of Companies C, H, L, & M under Major Simeon Brown.

This organization was adjusted or changed as needed throughout the Regiment's existence. Less than one month after its organization, on Saturday, October 11, 1862, most of the Sixth Michigan Volunteer Cavalry Regiment was formed on the parade field and mustered into federal service. Two days later, Companies F and K were sworn in and all the officers were formally commissioned. As part of the national army, they could now be ordered to proceed to war at any time.[13]

There were distractions and changes which occurred during the first weeks in camp. A rumor had circulated concerning pay-offs to Congressman Kellogg for commissions in the regiment. This was answered by the officers, and especially George Gray, with statements dated September 23 which were published in the Grand Rapids Eagle condemning the rumors and those who started them. [14]

Changes in the regimental staff took place as well. Adjutant Lyman E. Patten, brother of Quartermaster Charles H. Patten, resigned to become a Sutler – one of the few honest Sutlers to serve the army. He was replaced by Hiram Hale of Battle Creek,

COLONEL GEORGE GRAY
Photo courtesy of the Grand Rapids History &
Special Collections, Archives, Grand Rapids Public Library,
Grand Rapids, Michigan

who was commissioned on October 15. With George Gray being appointed Colonel, the position of Lieutenant-Colonel remained open until October 30, when Russell A. Alger, a Major in the Second Michigan Cavalry until three days before, was commissioned as Lieutenant-Colonel in the Sixth. Alger was an ambitious lawyer and businessman who brought intellect and experience to the regiment. [15]

Sickness hampered the Sixth at first, with many cases of colds and bronchitis brought on by exposure and close living conditions which the men were not used to. A hospital was set up in a house close to camp by Surgeon Daniel Weare of Pentwater. Doctor Weare, an excellent physician, had assistants who came and went, but despite his age and the harsh conditions he had to work in, he stayed with the regiment during its entire existence. Most men recovered from their illnesses, but a few did not. Private Andrew Conkling of Wyoming died on October 26, becoming Company B's first fatality.[16]

Stephen S. N. Greeley was the regimental Chaplain, and the only one the Sixth Cavalry would have. He had been the Pastor of the First Congregational Church in Grand Rapids. Greeley was kindly, caring, and giving of himself. On Sundays, weather permitting, the regiment would form up on the parade field in a hollow square and Chaplain Greeley would stand in the center to give his sermon. Many people from town came to camp to attend services with the soldiers.[17]

Drill continued and expanded to include Squadrons (two companies), Battalions (four companies), and finally the entire regiment. During this time most of the men, especially those who lived away from Grand Rapids, took short leaves and went home to say farewell to friends and family. Some men decided to marry their sweethearts before they left for war and uncertain fates. In September, early into the encampment, William Whitney went back to Wayland Township and married Lovina McBride. After the muster-in ceremony, Oscar Stout traveled to Courtland Township to exchange vows with his girl, Elizabeth Ann Benham. Others, like Allen Pease, Stephen Stowe, and George Patten, who already had families, took a few days to spend with their loved ones before departing.[18]

In the later part of November, after two months of training, the Sixth was completing its preparations for war. On November 26, Governor Blair sent a telegram to Major General Henry Halleck in Washington telling him that he had two regiments of Cavalry (5th & 6th), a regiment of Infantry (26th), and a battery of artillery (9th) ready to go, and asked where they should be sent. Halleck responded the same day and told Blair to send them all to Washington, D.C.[19]

On November 29, Miss Rebecca Richmond of Grand Rapids recorded in her diary that "The officers of the cavalry regiments gave a grand ball last evening at Luce's Hall." Miss Richmond undoubtedly danced with Peter Weber that night, as they had been longtime friends and corresponded during Weber's earlier service. Rebecca's cousin, who lived in Monroe, Michigan, met a cavalryman that very month who would become her husband. Her cousin was Elizabeth Bacon, and the cavalryman was Captain George A. Custer, who was destined to command the Michigan Cavalry Brigade, of which the Sixth would be a part. [20]

Departure for the regiment was close at hand, yet last minute volunteers still appeared. Among them was twenty-seven year old Elliott M. Norton, who left his home in Kalamazoo County in late November to enlist in Company B. Norton was an able man, and learned quickly. Drill was conducted as much as possible, and with greater intensity, especially for the newer men. Colonel Joseph R. Smith, an old Mexican War veteran who had mustered-in the regiment in October, returned to Grand Rapids on December 5, from his headquarters in Detroit, to administer the oath to the recent recruits.[21]

In the chill, early morning hours of Wednesday, December 10, 1862, the Sixth Michigan Cavalry Regiment marched on foot down the ridge and through the northern part of the still slumbering town to the rail station on the corner of Leonard Street and Plainfield Avenue. The horses and equipment were transported separately, under the watchful eyes of the company and regimental Quartermasters. The regiment initially tried to have each company mounted on the same colored horses (Blacks, Browns, Bays, Greys, etc.). Like the command structure, it wouldn't last very long, and never be the same again. No arms had yet been issued. Otherwise, the Sixth was fully equipped and ready to go. Departure for the front was not like the glorious send-off the Third Michigan Infantry had been given, yet it was acceptable to the men. A difficult and unpleasant job lay ahead, and the country had learned that sending men to war wasn't something to celebrate.[22]

Following is a list of Privates who were original members of Company B, Sixth Michigan Volunteer Cavalry Regiment, with their home towns or places of enlistment.[23]

Ackley, Newton – Newaygo
Batson, Charles – Alpine
Baxter, Solon – Grand Rapids
Bentley, Solon – Grand Rapids
Bowman, Lewis – Jamestown
Brown, Ezra – Blendon
Campbell, Archibald – Worth
Caywood, David – Alpine
Church, Isaac – Jamestown
Clark, Isaac – Jamestown
Clark, Orozene – Jamestown
Clay, Henry – Paris
Cole, Garrett – Wyoming
Colton, Alva – Paris
Conkling, Andrew – Wyoming
Cronkright, James – Jamestown
Cunningham, Philip – Brighton
Curry, Enoch – Brighton
Felton, Smith – Georgetown
Fuller, Daniel – Newaygo
Fuller, John – Newaygo
Gay, James – Newaygo
Glazier, Calvin – Newaygo
Gooch, Horace – Dayton
Gorman, Thomas – Big Rapids
Green, John – Jamestown
Green, Nathan – Big Rapids
Green, William – Grand Rapids
Greenman, Martin – Kellogville
Griffith, Gilbert – Jamestown
Gross, Frank – Algoma
Haist, Jacob – Big Rapids
Hall, John – Blendon

Hammond, Alfred – Wyoming
Howe, George – Blendon
Johnson, Nelson – Cortland Center
Johnson, Perley – Alpine
Kettle, Frederick – Alpine
Lewis, James – Georgetown
Lorsey, Charles – Deerfield
Lowe, William – Big Rapids
McCollister, Henry – Grand Rapids
McGowan, Thomas – Newaygo
Marsac, Lewis – Algoma
Martin, Alonzo – Wyoming
Mayfield, Oakland – Paris
Merrill, James – Algoma
Mitchell, William – Big Rapids
Molloy, John – Grand Rapids
Monroe, William – Blendon
Moss, William – Grand Rapids
Munson, David – Grand Rapids
Neal, Flavius – Alpine
Neal, James – Alpine
Newton, John – Coopersville
Norton, Augustus – Cooper
Norton, Elliott – Cooper
Pease, Allen – Grand Rapids
Pelton, Francis – Byron
Rogers, Remus – Algoma
Rossell, Abram – Grand Rapids
Runnels, Curtis – Algoma
Rust, David – Jamestown
Seely, Harvey – Big Rapids
Sharp, George – Sparta
Sliter, Josiah – Wyoming

Smith, Harvey – Wyoming
Stewart, Daniel – Wyoming
Stewart, Henry W. – Wyoming
Stout, Oscar – Courtland
Stowe, Stephen – Wayland
Trumbley, Benjamin – Muskegon
Tuffs, William – Jamestown
Wait, Justus – Blendon
Waite, Walter – Blendon
Watkins, Charles – Grand Rapids
Webster, James – Newaygo
Welch, Henry – Paris
Whitney, Edwin – Wayland
Whitney, William – Wayland

NOTES

1   Adjutant General's Office of Michigan. *Record of Service of Michigan Volunteers in the Civil War 1861-1865, Volume 36.* (Kalamazoo: Ihling Bro.s & Everard, 1905) 1. Hereafter cited as RSMV-36.

2   United States War Department. *War of the Rebellion: A compilation of the Official Records of the Union and Confederate Armies,* 70 Volumes in 4 series (Washington, D.C.: U.S. Government Printing Office, 1880-1891) Series III, Vol. II, 281 (Correspondence, Orders, Reports, & Returns). Acts of Congress listed in General Orders #91 from the Adjutant General's Office of the War Department dated July 29, 1862. Public Act #166, Section 11, passed on July 17, 1862. Citations from the Official Records will hereafter cited as OR with Series, Volume, Part (Where applicable), and Page; James H. Kidd, *Personal Recollections of a Cavalryman* (1908; reprint, Grand Rapids, Michigan: Black Letter Press, 1969) 30-31, 35-43; RSMV-36, 1.

3   RSMV-36.

4   RSMV-36, 107, 127, 133-135, 144, 147, 149; Civil War Compiled Military Service Records for Daniel and Henry W. Stewart, (Enlistment Documents) Records of the Adjutant General's Office, Record Group 94, National Archives, Washington, D.C.

5   RSMV-36, 146; Kidd, *Recollections,* 50.

6   RSMV-36, 1,146; 1860 U.S. Census, Kent County, Michigan, Grand Rapids 3rd Ward, p 111, National Archives Microfilm M653, Roll 550; C.S. Williams, *Grand Rapids Directory, City Guide and Business Mirror, Vol. 1, 1859-1860,* (Grand Rapids, P.G. Hodenpyl, 1859), 27, 108; OR, Series III, Vol. 2, 281, PA 166, Sect 8.

7   Kidd, *49-50.* These designations omitted the letter J, which was considered the same as the number 13.

8   Philip St. George Cooke, *Cavalry Tactics: or Regulations for the Instruction, Formations, and Movements of the Cavalry of the Army and Volunteers of the United States, Vol. 1 (*1862; reprint, Mattituck, N.Y.: J.M. Carroll & Company, 1999).

9   *Detroit Advertiser & Tribune,* September 23, 1862, 2; Kidd, 47.

10   RSMV-36, 36, 46, 77, 79, 81, 90, 92, 103, 106, 110, 11, 117, 125, 128, 138; Kidd, 67.

11   Kidd, 48; Regimental Order Book for the 6th Michigan Cavalry, Records of the Adjutant general's Office, Record Group 94, National Archives, Washington, D.C. Hereafter cited as Order Book. Equipment would have included McClellan saddles or variations, bridles, shoes, harness, brushes, farrier tools, etc.

12   Kidd, 51-53; Williams, 1859-60 G.R. Directory, 112;   William O. Lee, *Personal and Historical Sketches and Facial History of and by Members of the Seventh Regiment Michigan Volunteer Cavalry 1862-1865,* (Detroit, 7th Michigan Cavalry Association, 1902), 22-25.

13   RSMV-36; Order Book.

14   Detroit Advertiser & Tribune, October 18, 1862, 4.

15   RSMV-36, 1, 14; Kidd, 54, 55, 58.

16   RSMV-36, 36, 146; Kidd, 60.

17   RSMV-36, 61; Kidd, 56.

18   Kidd, 55, 57; Statement by William B. Whitney, Civil War Pension File SC-896801, Records of the Veterans Administration, Record Group 15, National Archives, Washington, D.C.; Marriage Record of Oscar Stout and Elizabeth Benham, 23 Oct.

1862, Vol. 3, p 149, Kent County Clerk's Office, Kent County Bldg., Grand Rapids, Mi.

19 OR, Series III, Vol. II, 880.

20 Z.Z. Lydens, Ed., The Story of Grand Rapids, (Grand Rapids, Mi.: Kregel Publications, 1967) 588-590; Kidd, 233; Gregory J.W. Urwin, Custer Victorious, (Rutherford, N.J.: Fairleigh Dickenson University Press, 1983) 55, 99.

21 RSMV-36, 102; Civil War Compiled Military Service Record for Elliott M. Norton, Record Group 94, National Archives, Washington, D.C.; Detroit Advertiser & Tribune, December 4, 1862, 1.

22 RSMV-36, 3; Kidd, 48, 69-70.

23 RSMV-36 & RSMV-40, 145; It appears that the company was organized in alphabetical order, in squads and platoons. Example: The seventh and eighth squads made up fourth platoon, consisting of men with names beginning with R and going to the end. This would explain why their experiences at the beginning of active operations were similar.

WASHINGTON, D.C. – GUARDING THE CAPITAL

Rolling through Detroit, Toledo, Cleveland, Pittsburg, and changing stations at Baltimore, the Sixth Michigan Cavalry arrived in Washington in parts between Sunday the fourteenth and Tuesday the sixteenth of December. For many of the men, it was the first time they ever rode on a train and traveled so far from home. They were housed temporarily in barracks near the station. Five days later they marched to a camp at the foot of Meridian Hill where it met Seventh Street, named Smith Park. The ground was unsuitable, much like the first camp by the river in Grand Rapids. Set up in a grove of trees with mud all around, the conditions caused many cases of colds and bronchitis among the men. On the day after a rather dismal Christmas, camp was moved up and along the hill to a much better location close to Fourteenth Street. Sheds were built for the horses, while the men lived in tents. Named "Camp Gray," the Sixth Michigan settled in for what was rumored to be a long stay as guards for the capital.[1]

After camp was set up, company and regimental drill began again. Men settled into a routine of drill, guard duty, parades, and work details. Reveille was changed to 6am on the regimental schedule, followed immediately by stable call before breakfast. When not on duty, and allowed a rare pass, troopers took in the local points of interest – both good and

FRANCIS W. KELLOGG
MEMBER OF CONGRESS

Photo Courtesy of the State Archives of Michigan

bad. Chaplain Greeley had enough influence on the troops to keep visits to the less reputable establishments to a minimum. As it was customary for new arrivals to pay their respects to the Commander-in-Chief, Congressman Kellogg took the

officers of the Sixth to meet President Lincoln. After intro-
ducing each of the officers, Kellogg boasted of a supposed
intention on their part to capture the rebel cavalry leader
J.E.B. Stuart. Lincoln replied with a grin, "Gentlemen, I can
assure you that it would give me much greater pleasure to
see Jeb Stuart in captivity than it has given me to see you." [2]

Company B had its numbers reduced at this time. Six men
of the Big Rapids contingent were transferred to Company D,
with the notable exception of Harvey Seely. Private Hammond
had been left in Detroit because he was too ill to continue to
Washington, and was eventually discharged from the service.
Winter arrived, and though not as severe as a Michigan Winter,
it still had its affects on men living close together in tents in
a growing, transient city. A wide variety of illnesses struck
down normally healthy men – from bronchitis, mumps, and
measles, to pleurisy and worse. Allen Pease, Edwin Whitney,
Elliott Norton, Stephen Stowe, and Wash Stewart all spent time
in Campbell Hospital, but recovered and returned to duty in
a few weeks. Others never did recover, and were eventually
transferred to the invalid corps or discharged from service and
sent home. Some were even less fortunate. Forty-three-year-
old Private Isaac Clark of Company B died on December 30. [3]

It didn't take long for the uniqueness of being in the capital
to wear off, and the drudgery of soldiering set in. Tennessee
born Mrs. Gray, in company with Mrs. Alger, visited their hus-
bands and helped boost morale for the officers. Enlisted
men, unable to have their wives with them, would visit the
various sites around the capital, but needed a pass to leave
camp. Displaying the traditional attitude of American volunteers which existed since the French and Indian Wars, they felt
this violated their personal rights as free men. Most of them
handled the restrictions, boredom, and loneliness with stoic

grace, but some chose another solution. On January 25, 1863, Company B suffered its first desertions – Privates Webster and Curry.[4]

In mid-January, the Sixth was issued 1840 and 1860 model cavalry sabers and Colt Army revolving pistols. A month later, rifles and carbines were issued to the men. Ordnance Bureau records for the first quarter of 1863 show breech-loading, single shot Burnside carbines were issued to companies B, F, I, K, L, and M. Four companies, A, D, E, and H, received the new Spencer seven-shot repeating rife. Companies C and G have no record of issues at all for the first six months of 1863, which indicates the weapons were probably redistributed after issue. There were enough Spencer rifles in the regiment to have at least one man in four armed with them.[5]

Just after the shoulder-fired weapons were issued, Companies I and M were detached for service in the lower Shenandoah Valley. They would remain there for more than a year. To mask the squadron's move, a rumor was circulated that they were going out on a scout, and would return in a few days.[6]

The Sixth was just beginning to become familiar with their weapons when they were sent out on their first mission. Orders were received in the evening on February 26 to prepare to march. In the early morning hours, the Sixth rode out of camp and over Long Bridge into Virginia. As they departed, an incessant rain began to fall. Riding until dawn, they were joined by the Fifth Michigan Cavalry. Continuing on, they passed through Alexandria and headed west to Centerville, arriving as night fell. [7]

A long, wet night was passed, and at six the next morning, three more regiments joined them to form a large brigade under the command of Sir Percy Wyndham, a foppish, English adventurer. They pushed on to Warrenton and just beyond, where they spent another tense night experiencing picket duty for the first time. Next day they continued the march to Falmouth, where the Army of the Potomac was camped and supplies could be found. Across the Rappahannock River, on the heights above Fredericksburg, lay the Confederate Army of Northern Virginia.[8]

Resting on the fourth day, the expedition drew rations and forage. During this scout, as it was called, the men learned hard lessons about marching, conserving rations, and camping. Next morning, Wyndham directed his column north, back to Washington. Maintaining a relentless pace, the ride ended two days later, leaving the regiment virtually dismounted. Horses were so used up it took nearly two weeks for many of them to recover – if they could recover. Some were ruined permanently. Men were also left exhausted, and wondering what they had accomplished. It was a miserable, yet valuable introduction to active operations.[9]

Cavalry was the busiest branch of the army. Tasks assigned to the horsemen were numerous and never-ending. Carrying messages, scouting, patrolling, screening, escorting supply trains or headquarters units, acting as military police on rare occasions, and picking up stragglers on the march were among the various duties. Men took care of themselves, and their horses and equipment as best they could. Usually the horses came first. Left with little time for rest on active operations, horse soldiers learned to eat, sleep, and live in the saddle.[10]

On March 11, another scout was taken into Fairfax County, Virginia led by another foreign adventurer - Hungarian born Brigadier General Julius Stahel. He was given command of the cavalry division after Wyndham was relieved. Horses and men who were fit enough participated in the three day mission, returning on the fourteenth. Again the ride accomplished little, although this time the horses finished in better shape.[11]

As the Sixth was leaving on the scout to Falmouth on February 27, ten companies of the Seventh Michigan Cavalry, under Colonel William Mann, arrived in Washington from Grand Rapids. It was brigaded with the Fifth and Sixth Regiments under the command of Brigadier General Joseph Copeland, the recently promoted former commander of the Fifth Michigan. After the Seventh was issued weapons, the brigade was sent out to Fairfax County again. On March 24, the Sixth headed across the Potomac to Bailey's Crossroads, between the capitol and Centerville. Heading west into Loudon County, they scouted through Middleburg and on to Ashby's Gap. Finding nothing, they marched back to Fairfax Court House in a seasonably late snowfall. From there, the regiment was dispersed by Battalions along a line following Difficult Creek to perform picket duty as part of the capital's outer defenses. Five companies, including Company B, established a base about two miles south of Vienna, called Camp Meeting Hill. While the Sixth set up temporary residence in Virginia, their semi-permanent camps and equipment in Washington were packed in wagons and moved to Fairfax County, where they would remain for another three months. [12]

As it was with the entire regiment, Company B lost a number of men to illness and transfers during this period. Second Lieutenant Charles Storrs was transferred to Company G on the sixteenth of March, and First Lieutenant Warren Comstock resigned for health reasons on the twenty-third. Regimental Order number 44, dated April 1, 1863, promoted First-Sergeant

Daniel Powers to First Lieutenant. Second Lieutenant Charles Bolza was passed over. Why this was done is unknown, but Powers must have demonstrated ability for higher authority and responsibility. Governor Blair had to confirm the appointment before Powers could be officially commissioned, but he assumed the rank and duties immediately. Storrs position remained open.[13]

There were changes for the Non-Commissioned Officers as well. Corporal John Molloy followed Storrs to Company G in May with a promotion as First Sergeant. Corporal John Maxfield had been promoted to Sergeant at the beginning of 1863 when Edwin Robinson was reduced to Private. Maxfield was then discharged for disability in April. Corporal James Keater was also discharged for disability that month. Promoted in their places were David Caywood, Allen Pease, and Edwin Whitney. Quartermaster Sergeant George Patten took Power's place as First Sergeant, and Nelson Thomas moved into Patten's position. Corporal Harvey Potter was promoted to Sergeant, and Private Elliott Norton was jumped over all the other Corporals in the company to Sergeant. Norton's ability and ambition were recognized early, and would prove to be of value to Company B and the regiment.[14]

Corporal Dorr Skeels became so ill in February that he spent over a year, off and on, in the hospital before being transferred to the Veteran Reserve Corps in the summer of 1864. After being reduced to Private in January, Edwin Robinson was detailed to the Brigade Ambulance Corps to the end of 1863, and then as an orderly at Brigade Headquarters until the Spring of 1865. Bugler Calvin Glazier was permanently detailed to the regimental band. Privates Henry Clay, Garrett Cole, Martin Greenman, John Hall, Nelson Johnson, Benjamin Trumbly, and Justus Wait were all discharged for disability or in hospitals awaiting discharge. Of the ninety-nine

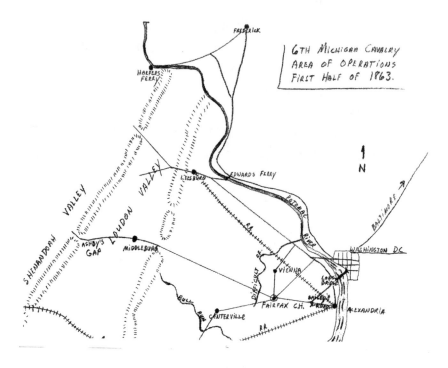

men who started out in Company B, twenty-four were permanently lost for various reasons in that first six months. With others out sick temporarily or detailed away for other tasks, the company didn't have more than sixty men in the field at the end of June.[15]

In early April the Sixth Michigan again rode into Loudon County searching for Mosby and his men. Finding nothing, they returned to their camp on April 7. Awaiting First Sergeant George Patten were two letters from his wife Lydia, and one from his mother. He read the letters from his wife first, the more recent one describing how she had fallen ill. His mother's letter informed him that Lydia had died - on the very day he was promoted. Patten's young son was in the care of his parents back home in Alpine Township. He was devastated by the news, and his friend Daniel Powers did his best to console him.[16]

For most of the men in Company B, duty in Fairfax County was relatively pleasant and quiet. Occasionally, this tranquility was disturbed by brief encounters with rebel guerillas. On April 23, raiders captured Privates Solon Bentley and Lewis Bowman while they were searching for food from the local farmers beyond the picket line. They were taken first to Upperville, then marched on foot to Richmond and held there for a few days. Paroled and sent to a parole camp at Annapolis, Maryland, they were exchanged and returned to the company at Fairfax Court House on May 20.[17]

In early June, Mosby became more active in support of Lee's operations. Clashes with the guerillas increased. The Sixth Michigan lost Lieutenant-Colonel Alger on June 11, when Governor Blair appointed him to be Colonel of the Fifth Michigan. Major Thaddeus Foote assumed command of Alger's Battalion. On June 15, the Army of the Potomac arrived in the area of the cavalry camps, moving in pursuit of Lee's Army of Northern Virginia. The pickets were brought in, and the brigade was concentrated at Fairfax Court House. During this period, the Michigan horsemen were sent south to scout Warrenton Junction twice, each time finding nothing while hearing cannon firing to the west. On the second mission, they rode through the old Bull Run Battlefield, where the debris of war and half-buried bodies were still visible on the ground.[18]

On the twenty-fifth of June, with their camps broken down and ready to move, men of the Sixth Michigan Cavalry, and the Michigan Cavalry Brigade, moved out as part of the Army of the Potomac. Easy days of garrison and picket duty for the capital were over.[19]

NOTES

1   Eloise A. Haven, ed., *In the Steps of a Wolverine: The Civil War Letters of a Michigan Cavalryman*, (Kentwood, Mi.: Self-published, 2005) 6; *Grand Rapids Daily Eagle*, (Grand Rapids, Mi.) 11 Feb. 1863, 2.

2   Order Book, #24; Haven, 6-7; Kidd, 73-76.

3   RSMV-36, 33, 60, 62-64, 87, 95, 122 (Privates T. Gorman, N. Green, J. Haist, C. Lorsey, W. Lowe, W. Mitchell); Haven, 7; Civil War Compiled Military Service Records for Henry Stewart, Elliott Norton, Stephen Stowe, and Edwin Whitney (Hospital Records), Records of the Adjutant General's Office, Record Group 94, National Archives, Washington, D.C.

4   RSMV-36, 42, 146; Haven, 5; Kidd 84.

5   Haven, 8; Kidd, 76-78; Records of the Office of the Chief of Ordnance, Summary Statements of Quarterly Returns of Ordnance and Ordnance Stores on Hand in Regular and Volunteer Army Organizations, 1862-1867, 1870-1876, Record Group 156, National Archives Microfilm Series 1281, Roll 2, Vol. 2-3.

6   Haven, 10; Frederick A. Dyer, *A Compendium of the War of the Rebellion*, (Des Moines, Iowa: The Dyer Publishing Co. 1908) Vol. 3, 1273.

7   Kidd, 87-90.

8   ibid, 90-92, 94-95.

9   ibid, 95-96.

10   Gregory J.W. Urwin, *The United States Cavalry: An Illustrated History*, (Poole, Dorset, U.K.: Blandford Press, 1983) 114, 133.

11   Kidd, 96-100.

12   Haven, 12, 14-15; Kidd, 96-102; John Robertson (compiler), *Michigan in the War*, (Lansing, Mich.: W.S. George and Company, 1880) 573.

13   RSMV-36, 111; Haven, 17-18.

14   RSMV-36, 31, 79, 92, 96, 102, 106, 107, 110, 117, 138, 149; Haven, 17.

15   RSMV-36, 34, 35, 62, 64, 77, 125, 140, 144; Morning Reports of the Sixth Michigan Cavalry Regiment, entry 6, February 1863, Records of the Adjutant General's Office, Record Group 94, National Archives, Washington, D.C.; Civil War Compiled Military Service records for Edwin Robinson and Dorr Skeels (Notes on muster rolls), Records of the Adjutant General's Office, Record Group 94, National Archives, Washington, D.C.

16   Richard L. Hamilton, *Oh! Hast Thou Forgotten,* (Tucson, Az.: Self-published, 2008) 34; Haven, 16; Daniel H. Powers to his parents, April 9,1863, correspondence and diary in possession of David Van Dyke of Nappanee, Indiana.

17   Haven, 18, 22; Kidd, 101-103.

18   Kidd, 107, 109-112.

19   Ibid, 113.

GETTYSBURG – FIRST CAMPAIGN

Assigned as rear guard for the column, the Sixth Michigan Cavalry had to wait near Vienna, Virginia while the army marched past. Captains Peter Weber and James Kidd got permission to ride back to the vicinity of their old camp and say goodbye to the residents who had befriended them. After a pleasant visit and final farewells, the pair rode to a point where they thought they would find the regiment. Instead, they found the head of the column. Relaxing comfortably near the road, Weber and Kidd contentedly waited for their compatriots to catch up. It took all afternoon.[1]

Reaching the well rested pair near dusk, the regiment continued marching into the night. After crossing the Potomac at Edwards Ferry in the dark, they rode north into Maryland. Rain began to fall, and their guide got lost, but they kept going until a few hours before dawn. Stopping briefly to rest near Poolesville, the march resumed at first light. In the afternoon, the rain finally stopped and the sky began to clear as the column approached Frederick, Maryland. As the sun set, the light shone through the mist hanging over the countryside and created a spectacular, golden glow on the land, delighting many tired troopers. Frederick's citizens proved to be gracious and friendly, and the Sixth happily made camp for the night.[2]

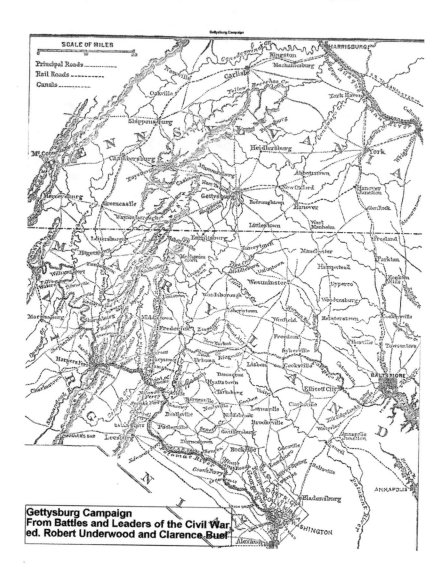

Gettysburg Campaign
From Battles and Leaders of the Civil War,
ed. Robert Underwood and Clarence Buel

On June 27, the Fifth and Sixth regiments rode toward Emmitsburg, searching for the Confederate Army, known to be somewhere nearby. They camped for the night just south of the town - two miles from the Pennsylvania line. Next morning, a Sunday, General Copeland led the column north, along the Emmitsburg road into Gettysburg, arriving in the afternoon.

The townspeople were very welcoming, and told of enemy troops marching through two days earlier. Camp was set up east of town, and a vigilant and nervous picket was kept for the night.[3]

On Monday, the command was informed of recent organizational changes. The Fifth, Sixth, and Seventh Michigan regiments were joined by the First Michigan Cavalry and Battery M, Second U.S. Artillery, and designated as the Second Brigade, Third Division, of the Cavalry Corps, Army of the Potomac. Informally, they would be known as the "Michigan Cavalry Brigade." General Copeland was replaced by newly appointed Brigadier General George A. Custer, a graduate of West Point and former staff officer from Ohio and Michigan. General Stahel was replaced by Brigadier General Judson Kilpatrick as commander of the Division. Copeland turned the command over to Colonel Gray and departed to report to Major General George Meade, the new commander of the Army of the Potomac.[4]

After Copeland left, the Fifth and Sixth went back to Emmitsburg while keeping patrols out to the east. Ordered to join First Brigade of the Division at Littlestown, Pennsylvania, the column slogged its way through the night, arriving at sunrise on June 30, in a rain shower. Patrols were sent in every direction. Reports came in telling of Confederate cavalry under General Jeb Stuart in the area. First Brigade rode to Hanover, in Stuart's path, while Company A of the Sixth, and the Fifth Michigan were ordered to scout roads to the southwest and southeast, in the general direction of Westminster. The nine remaining companies of the Sixth had a little time to tend their horses and attempt to have breakfast.[5]

A little later in the morning, a local resident came running into town saying there was a large force of Rebels a few miles away in the direction of Hanover. Colonel Gray ordered the tired and still hungry horse soldiers to mount up. In column of fours, they moved out accompanied by many citizens with shotguns trotting along with them, determined to join the fight. By that time, the rain had stopped.[6]

When the column was about two miles from Hanover, they encountered enemy skirmishers on their right, and probably heard the sounds of battle coming from Hanover. Gray led the Sixth off the road, through a wheat field, and up a slope to see what was in front of them. As they reached the crest, they saw a large body of Confederate cavalry a half-mile away supported by a two gun section of artillery. The artillery opened fire on them and forced them back down the slope to the road near Schwartz Schoolhouse. A second force of enemy cavalry then appeared on their right rear, shooting and preparing to charge them. Knowing his green and outnumbered regiment could not win a fight with rebel veterans, Gray ordered Captain Weber, his most experienced officer, with companies B and F, to fight a holding action while the rest of the Sixth

View of Mt. Pleasant from the Littlestown-Hanover Road.

continued to Hanover. Company F had another veteran in its ranks – Lieutenant Don Lovell. In 1861, Weber and Lovell had been Corporals together in Company A of the Third Michigan Infantry.[7]

Weber formed the squadron, numbering about 120 men, for defense in and around patches of woods back up on the ridge. He kept them mounted, as they had learned from General Cooke's manual. The First Virginia, part of Brigadier General Fitzhugh Lee's Confederate Cavalry Brigade, charged the Michigan troopers. Weber's men threw them back with a counter-charge, using their sabers, Burnside carbines and Colt revolvers. Those men with Spencer rifles found it too hard to shoot accurately while on horseback. The Virginians reformed and charged a second time, and the squadron again countered. A Rebel Lieutenant was captured during this action and some of the Michigan troopers were agitated to the point of wanting to

Schwartz Schoolhouse

shoot their prisoner. Lieutenant Powers came along, knocked down their weapons with his sword, and spared the captive officer.[8]

Fighting ebbed and flowed along the narrow lanes, in cultivated fields and thick woods on the high ground south of the Schwartz Schoolhouse on the Littlestown-Hanover road. Like many of the troopers, Powers had some close calls, including shots that took his hat off his head, and one that bent his scabbard and wounded his horse. A third charge was made by the Virginians, and the squadron countered, while drawing them away from the regiment's line of march toward Hanover. Lieutenant Powers, who commanded Company B while Captain Weber was in command of the squadron, moved some of his men into a patch of woods to rest the horses and reload. Before they could accomplish that, Sergeant Keyes yelled, "They are flanking us!" Seeing they were outnumbered by about five-to-one, and not sure if they had been spotted, Powers ordered his men "to retreat up the road a ways" and went back to find out. As he slowly made his way to a point where he could observe enemy movements, unseen rebel skirmishers ambushed him, killing his horse and taking him prisoner. He managed to throw his pistol into a field where his rebel captors couldn't find it, angering them. Just as they were about to abuse him, the Rebel Lieutenant he had rescued earlier, and who managed to escape shortly afterward, came up and saved him from harm.[9]

Daniel Stewart was in another group from Company B which included his son "Wash." Daniel had been wounded in the leg. In addition, both their horses had been shot at the start of the fight, but continued to carry them through two more charges. After driving the rebels away on the third charge, Stewart stated, "we hauled off and went down to a house...the rebs were all

Confederate view as they approached the 6th Michigan at first contact on Mt. Pleasant. The house belonged to the Neihafer family.

round us but not in sight. We rode into a piece of woods and lay there until near sundown." While hiding, they watched the enemy columns march by, about 250 yards away. As it started getting dark they were spotted, and "had just time to mount our horses and dig out when they began to shell the woods." Wash had to leave his horse, being too lame and hurt to continue. Many of the men lost equipment and personal possessions while fighting and eluding the enemy.[10]

During the fight, Weber's squadron lost about twenty men, most of them from Company B. Along with Lieutenant Powers, Corporals Caywood, McVean, and Whitney, plus Privates Gay, McGowen, Tuffs, Bentley, Harvey Smith, Stout, Stowe, Waite, and Watkins were taken prisoner. Private Ezra Brown was also wounded when captured. Bugler John Newton was missing and presumed a prisoner until he rejoined the company on July 4. Company F lost Sergeant Frank Konkle captured, Sergeant Averill wounded, and a few others who were scattered during the action.[11]

Captain Weber managed to disengage from Fitz Lee's Cavalry Brigade, aided in part by the Fifth Michigan, who had completed their scout towards Westminster and were approaching on the road from Littlestown. Cut off from the Sixth at Hanover, he rallied what remained of his squadron and rode most of the night to the North and East, along unfamiliar roads, and finally rejoined the regiment just before dawn on the first day of July. Despite his losses and rough handling by the rebels, Weber and his men had done a masterful job. They held back superior numbers of the enemy and allowed the Sixth to move unmolested to Hanover and participate in the battle. As the regiment approached the town, and in later fighting, they helped push the Confederate Brigade under Colonel John Chambliss farther away from the Hanover-Littlestown road to secure their communications with Corps and Army Headquarters, and kept Jeb Stuart from linking up with the Army of Northern Virginia.[12]

Forced away from Hanover, Stuart's command, with their recent captives herded along on foot, also marched through the night. Reaching Dover, Pennsylvania at sunrise on July 1, Stuart halted his columns and allowed them time to rest while he sent out scouts to find General Lee and his Army. Stuart was already burdened with captured federal supply wagons, and didn't want the additional problem of prisoners, so he paroled his captives at Dover, and moved on toward Carlisle. The parolees, led by Lieutenant Powers, were sent to a camp at Westchester, Pennsylvania to await exchange.[13]

After rejoining the regiment at Hanover, the remaining men of Company B were allowed to rest for much of the day.

This is where they first saw their new Brigade Commander, Brigadier General George Armstrong Custer. In the afternoon, they marched north by west, through Abbottstown, Hunterstown, and beyond before stopping for the night. Next day, July 2, they turned around and went back to Hunterstown with the Sixth in the lead. Finding the town occupied by Wade Hampton's Brigade of Confederate Cavalry, part of Stuart's command, the regiment deployed for battle. A brisk fight took place, but neither side gained any advantage while suffering casualties, especially during a charge by Company A of the Sixth. Afterward, the Michigan Brigade was ordered south to a crossroads known as Two Taverns. Men and horses again marched through most of the night, but were allowed to rest when they arrived.[14]

On the morning of July 3, the Brigade began to move toward the Round Tops south of Gettysburg when their orders were suddenly changed. Brigadier General David Gregg, who commanded the Second Cavalry Division, ordered Custer's Brigade to help him defend a vulnerable area on the opposite flank of the army. The Michigan Cavalry marched back to the North, with the Sixth again leading. As they arrived, Custer placed the Brigade along the Hanover Road facing west toward Gettysburg, and North toward the York Road, which were likely avenues of approach for enemy forces. Four companies of the Sixth were dismounted and put in line along a creek on the left flank , while four others were kept mounted and held near the artillery battery supporting the Brigade. This was Battery M of the Second U.S. Artillery Regiment, a regular Army unit commanded by First Lieutenant Alexander C.M. Pennington, a steady and professional officer of great ability and courage.[15]

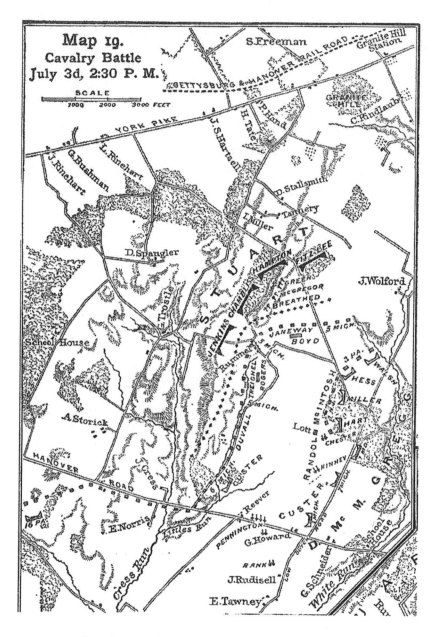

From Battles and Leaders of the Civil War, Ed. Robert
Underwood and Clarence Buel

To protect his flanks, Custer sent Company G, with Lieutenant Charles Storrs in command, out to the West along the Hanover Road. He also sent Peter Weber with Company B North along the Low Dutch Road. Both companies were under Weber's direction, and each went out about a mile-and-a-half. Weber had recently been informed of his impending promotion to Major, but had not yet been mustered into his new rank. He was promoted to replace Major Elijah Waters, who had resigned in May for health reasons. While his advancement was not yet official, and still wearing Captain's bars, Weber assumed the rank and title of Major.[16]

When Weber reached his position, he was able to observe Stuart's brigades marching from the York Road, past the Stallsmith farm, and into place along Cress Ridge near the Rummel farmhouse. He reported promptly to Custer. Soon after arriving on the ridge, Stuart had his artillery begin firing on the federal troops. Custer ordered Pennington and his battery to respond. In a short time, they forced Stuart's guns to cease fire and fall back. General Gregg arrived then to take personal command on the field. Close behind him was one of his brigades commanded by Colonel John McIntosh. For a short time, a lull in the action settled over the field. Kidd described what happened next. "Suddenly there burst upon the air the sound of that terrific cannonading that preceded Picket's charge. The earth quaked. The tremendous volume of sound volleyed and rolled across the intervening hills like reverberating thunder in a storm." While Lee's assault on the federal center was taking place a few miles to the West on Cemetery Ridge, Jeb Stuart was squaring off against Gregg and Custer on the Rummel Farm.[17]

Thanks to Weber, Custer knew what was in front of him, and he ordered the Fifth Michigan, armed with Spencer rifles, to advance as dismounted skirmishers. Aware of Weber's vantage point, the Confederates attacked and drove him and Company B back inside their own lines. There they joined with the Battalion defending the artillery, along with Storrs and Company G, who had also returned. Colonel Alger and his Fifth Michigan were slowly pushing the enemy back, but soon they were running out of ammunition. Not only did the Spencer rifles fire faster, they also ate up each soldier's allotted rounds faster. Realizing the federal fire was slackening, the Rebels began to advance. Weber told his men to be ready to charge.[18]

Just then, the Seventh Michigan entered the field and charged. They were held up by fences, which eventually caused the assault to fail. As the Seventh began to retire, the Rebels counter-attacked. A portion of the Fifth had managed to get to their horses, and met the enemy with a charge of their own, allowing the Seventh to fall back without interference. Seeing an opportunity, Stuart sent in the brigades of Wade Hampton and Fitzhugh Lee in a mounted charge intending to break the federal lines and drive them away. Generals Gregg and Custer then ordered the veteran First Michigan to charge in and stop

Weber's position on the Low Dutch Road near the Wolford farm, from where he observed Stuart's movements.

the Confederate attack. Aided by Pennington's guns, and portions of McIntosh's Brigade and the Fifth and Seventh Michigan regiments on the flanks, the First slammed into the attackers head-on. After some very desperate fighting, the rebel horsemen were forced to retreat. The lines were quickly reformed on both sides, and the wounded were collected from the field, but the fight had ended. The right flank and rear of the Army of the Potomac were secure. Stuart and his troopers moved off later in the day, harassed by McIntosh's brigade.[19]

By providing Custer with vital information about the enemy, Peter Weber and Company B played a major part in the battle, but didn't actually participate in the fighting. They had a good view of the action while standing ready, and suffered no casualties. With the battle won, the Brigade stayed on the field until dark, and then marched back to Two Taverns on the Baltimore Pike, camping for the night. Men got a brief rest before continuing to the next phase of the campaign.[20]

Pennington's guns were posted to the right, and Weber's squadron stood in support on the opposite side of the Hanover Road.

NOTES

1   Kidd, 113-114.

2   ibid, 114-116; Robertson, 573.

3   Kidd, 116-122; Robertson, 574.

4   Kidd, 122-124; OR, Series I, Vol. 27, Part 3, 373.

5   Kidd, 124-125: Robertson, 580 (Gray's report).

6   Kidd, 125-127; Haven, 35; Daniel Stewart to Margaret Murray, July 24, 1863, Regional History Collections, File A-284, East Bldg., East Campus, Western Michigan University, Kalamazoo, Michigan.

7   Kidd, 126-127; Robertson, 580; RSMV-36, 86; RSMV-3, 121.

8   Daniel H. Powers to his Parents, 19 July 1863, Diary and Correspondence in possession of David Van Dyke and Family, Nappanee, Indiana; Stewart Letter of July 24, 1863.

9   Powers Letter of July 19, 1863.

10   Stewart Letter of July 24, 1863.

11   Grand Rapids Daily Eagle, July 25, 1863, 1; RSMV-36; RSMV-40, 145; OR, Series I, Vol. 27, Part 1, 999 (Custer's Report); Memorandums from Prisoner of War Records, taken from Civil War Compiled Military Service Records for individuals involved, Records of the Adjutant General's Office, Record Group 94, National Archives, Washington, D.C.

12   Kidd, 127-128, 132-133; Haven, 32; Stewart Letter July 24, 1863; Robertson, 580; OR, 999 (Custer).

13   Haven 35; Memorandums from Prisoner of War Records (See note 11).

14 Kidd, 133-135; OR, Series I, Vol. 27, Pt. 1, 999 (Custer).

15 Kidd, 135-140; Robertson, 580-581 (Gray), 582-584 (Custer).

16 RSMV-36, 146; Kidd, 140, 146-147; Robertson, 583.

17 Kidd, 142, 143, 145.

18 ibid, 146, 148; Robertson, 583.

19 Kidd, 148-155; Robertson, 583-584; OR, Series I, Vol. 27, Pt. 1, 956-958 (Gregg's report).

20 Kidd, 161; Robertson, 584.

PURSUIT – PUSHING
BACK TO VIRGINIA

On the morning of July 4, the Michigan Brigade linked up with First Brigade of the Third Cavalry Division near Emmitsburg. This is where most of the men saw their Division Commander, Brigadier General Judson Kilpatrick, for the first time. Kilpatrick ordered his regimental commanders to draw three days rations and prepare to go after the enemy's trains. They were to harass and slow them down as much as possible while the rest of the Army marched to catch up. Before the cavalrymen got on the road to start their pursuit, a torrential rain began to fall.[1]

Turning West on the road to Waynesboro, Pennsylvania, Kilpatrick's Division marched up South Mountain in the direction of the road from Fairfield, on which Confederate wagon trains were moving. As it began to get dark, the rain slacked off, and the column continued on with the Fifth and Sixth Michigan regiments in the lead. Near midnight, while marching along a narrow part of the road near Monterey Gap with the mountain rising on the right and falling off sharply on the left, the men were fired on by the enemy. One lone artillery piece, supported by a small band of determined Marylanders blocked their way. Custer ordered the two lead regiments dismounted and formed in line on either side of the road, with the Sixth on the right, to sweep away opposition along the road. Stumbling through tangled undergrowth, and up and down gullies in the dark, the men moved along by sound and feel rather than sight. Only the flashes of guns could be seen. Pushing on to a stream running high and fast because of the rains, the Michigan men were held up for a short time at a bridge before forcing a crossing and clearing the road. At this point Custer ordered a mounted regiment from First Brigade to charge, and the enemy resistance was broken. Kilpatrick's command rode on and captured or destroyed a portion of Lieutenant General Richard Ewell's Second Corps trains.[2]

In the darkness and confusion of the fighting, Quartermaster Sergeant Nelson Thomas was wounded in the left hand and hip, and taken prisoner. Held for only two days, he was paroled and sent to a hospital in Gettysburg, and later to Philadelphia. He was the only casualty from Company B in this action.[3]

After the fight, exhausted Michigan troopers got back in the saddle and made a night march, which had started to become routine. Men put their chins in their chests and fell asleep, and the horses plodded along at their own, individual paces. Soon the column became an ambling, slumbering mob. When it got light, the men awoke and found themselves among others they hadn't started with. They quickly sorted themselves out and reformed their companies. After stopping to have breakfast, the troopers were able to see some of the captured wagons, and talk to prisoners who had fought them in the darkness.[4]

Pushing on, Third Cavalry Division marched southwest through Cavetown and on to Smithsburg, with Stuart's cavalry pecking at them along the way. At Smithsburg they were attacked by Confederates in strength and forced to retire to Boonsborough after dark. Next morning, Kilpatrick turned the captured wagons and prisoners over to the proper authorities and moved on to Hagerstown. In the afternoon First Brigade reached Hagerstown at the same time as the lead elements of

Lee's Army, and drove them back, holding the road open for the Michigan Brigade. As they got to the town, Custer turned them left and started on the road to Williamsport, where Lee's Army was intending to cross the Potomac. The river was running very high after the recent rains, and federal commanders hoped the Confederates might be trapped against it and forced to surrender.[5]

With Sixth Michigan marching at the rear of the column, the brigade advanced toward Williamsport and soon made contact with rebel forces defending the town. At the same time, pressure was building on First Brigade as more of the Confederate Army arrived at Hagerstown. Fighting back-to-back between two enemy forces, both brigades of Third Division fought its way down the road toward Williamsport. Opposing the Michigan men was Brigadier General John Imboden with his own cavalry brigade, and wagon drivers for the Army of Northern Virginia organized into detachments, ably supported by several batteries of artillery. As the day wore on, Third Division was pushed into an increasingly smaller area and in danger of being destroyed. Night finally arrived, and with help from Brigadier General John Buford's First Cavalry Division, Third Division slipped away. After another night march, they arrived back at Boonsborough and were allowed to rest through all of July 7. Exhausted men and horses barely noticed the cloudburst that soaked them.[6]

With Lee's Army trapped on the left bank of the Potomac, Stuart established a cavalry screen in front of Confederate positions around Williamsport. On July 8, Buford's First Division and Kilpatrick's Third Division attacked Stuart's troopers in a dismounted fight northwest of Boonsborough, along the Hagerstown road. Deployed along a rail fence in front of a patch of woods, the Sixth Michigan skirmished over an open field with rebels behind a stone wall. After some time, with neither side gaining any advantage, a staff officer appeared and gave orders, supposedly from General Kilpatrick, to retreat. Dutifully obeying the order, the line fell back away from the rail fence and through the woods. Rebels quickly occupied the position just vacated, and continued into the woods behind the Michigan troopers. It was about this time they began to wonder why they had been ordered to fall back when there was no obvious reason to do so. Learning General Kilpatrick had given no such order, the gullible Yankees realized they had been tricked by a brave and resourceful rebel in a federal uniform. At this point Peter Weber yelled "Forward, my men," and led some embarrassed and peeved Michiganders in a charge that recovered all the lost ground, and continued until darkness halted their pursuit.[7]

For the next two days, the Michigan Brigade rested at Boonsborough, and wondered why the Army of the Potomac was not hurrying to take advantage of the enemy being strung out on the roads and trapped against the river. Cavalry commanders felt the war could be ended if the infantry would come up and press the enemy hard.[8]

Early on July 11, the Michigan Brigade was part of an attack on Hagerstown. Deploying several sharpshooters, the enemy forced the federal troopers to dismount and advance. Fighting degenerated to skirmishing, and ended when it got dark. On the following day, the Confederates fell back from the town and established a perimeter around Williamsport, allowing Hagerstown to be occupied by federal troops. July 13 was spent resting, getting a decent meal, and preparing to move on the enemy next day.[9]

Advancing at first light, scouts discovered the Rebels had withdrawn during the night. Kilpatrick and the Third Cavalry division pursued slowly through abandoned enemy positions to the river at Williamsport, and watched the last Confederates cross. Frustrated, Kilpatrick pushed hard to get to another crossing site he'd been informed of five miles down river at Falling Waters. The Sixth Michigan Cavalry was in front, with Peter Weber's Battalion leading. Due to muddy conditions that wore out horses, and rebel stragglers who needed to be guarded and taken to a collection point, the column became smaller and strung out along the way. Riding on Falling Waters Road, Companies B and F pulled off into a patch of woods to the right. Custer and Kilpatrick were riding just behind Weber's squadron and wanted to see what was in front of them. Beyond the woods was a large open field gradually sloping up to high ground commanding the road. On the high ground were Confederate troops behind earthworks consisting of about a half-dozen mounds of packed dirt. They appeared to be resting, and had stacked their arms.[10]

Custer ordered Weber to dismount his men and advance as skirmishers. As they were preparing to move out, Kilpatrick

Where companies B & F began the charge, coming up the hill toward the camera. Falling Waters Road is on the right.

countermanded the order, and told Weber to charge the enemy position. Obeying the order, he got his men back in the saddle, and lined up. Weber had earlier confided to Captain James Kidd of Company E, that he wanted to make at least one saber charge during the war. Now he had his chance. There were twenty-nine men in line from Company B, and about the same number in Company F. Weber placed himself in front, had the men close up and draw their sabers, and gave the order "Forward!" Slowly they emerged from the woods with the road on their left. Once all of the troopers had cleared the trees, Weber ordered them to the trot as they swept up the hill.[11]

On their objective, Confederates Major General Henry Heth and Brigadier General J. Johnston Pettigrew, stood near the Donnelly house while observing the cavalry coming up, and initially thought it was their own troops. Behind the mounds of earth, Archer's Brigade was resting, with most of their arms stacked and unloaded. Archer himself had been captured on July 1 at Gettysburg, along with many of his soldiers. On July 3, they had been decimated in Pickett's charge. The brigade was now commanded by Lieutenant-Colonel S.G. Shepard of the Seventh Tennessee Infantry Regiment. Just behind them and a little to the left, and not seen by Kilpatrick, was Pettigrew's Brigade of North Carolinians, who had the same experiences as Archer's Brigade. Across the road from Donnelly's, was Brockenbrough's Brigade of Virginians. All of them were exhausted. Some had gone to sleep on the ground.[12]

Objective of the charge.
Looking toward the Donnelly House and heights occupied by Archer's Brigade.

When Major Weber was about 150 yards from the enemy, he ordered the charge. With a yell the Michigan men pounded up over the crest of the hill and rode among the startled Confederates. Many Michigan troopers called for surrender, and the Rebels around them stood with their hands in the air. When they realized how few Yankees there were, they went for their guns. Some Southerners grabbed their unloaded rifles and began using them like clubs, or started loading them. Others who couldn't get to their guns picked up fence rails or anything else they could find to use as weapons. Weber's men began swinging their sabers and firing their pistols as fast as they could. Their charge had initially been made on the First Tennessee. As the fight progressed, it moved to the right and diminished as it fell upon the Thirteenth Alabama, and played out as it reached the Seventh and Fourteenth Tennessee Regiments. Behind Shepard's troops, some of

Pettigrew's Brigade saw what was happening and moved up to join the fight. All this happened very quickly. In only a few minutes, the federals began to be overwhelmed, and those who remained made a dash back down the hill to their own lines. As they attempted to escape, the rebels continued to shoot them down.[13]

Just as the remnants of Weber's squadron limped back to the woods at the bottom of the hill, the rest of the Sixth Michigan arrived on the scene. Custer had them dismount and deploy as skirmishers. A heavy fire fight began in which more men from the regiment were killed and wounded. Captain David Royce, commanding Company D, was killed and Captain James Kidd of Company E was wounded in the foot. Soon, Kilpatrick was able to bring up all of the Division and press the Confederates. An attack, which coincided with a rebel withdrawal to the pontoon bridge at Falling Waters, brought the battle to an end. Many Confederates were taken prisoner, and the colors of three Virginia regiments of Brockenbrough's Brigade were captured.[14]

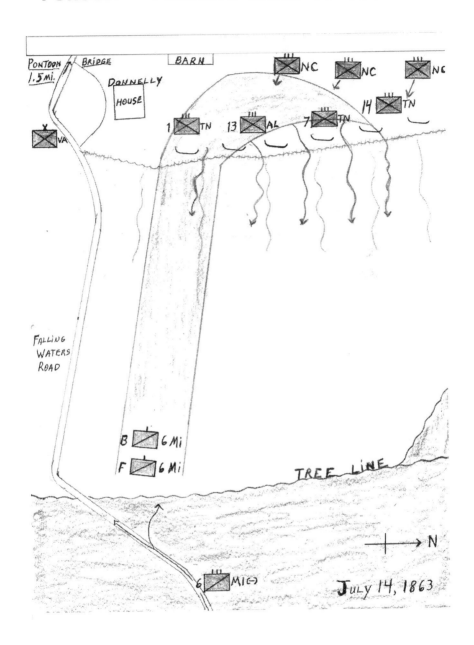

"Charge of the 6th Michigan Cavalry over the rebel earthworks near Falling Waters"
Drawing by Alfred R. Waud Library of Congress

Company B was nearly destroyed at Falling Waters. Killed in action were Acting Major Peter Weber, Second Lieutenant Charles Bolza in actual command of the company, First Sergeant George Patten, who was recently widowed and left an orphan at home, Sergeant Harvey Potter, and Privates Batson, Gooch, Martin, Mayfield, F. Neal, Pelton, Rossel, and Sliter. Wounded were Sergeant Keyes and Privates Campbell, Colton, McCollister, and Rogers. Rogers would later die of his wounds. Missing and presumed captured were Corporal Platt and Privates Baxter, G. Griffith, Lewis, and Marsac. Platt and Lewis would die as prisoners of war. Griffith disappeared.[15]

Only seven men from Company B came out of the charge unhurt, and they all had very close calls. During the fight, a rebel was about to shoot Private Wash Stewart, but Stewart slashed the man's arm with his saber, causing him to drop his rifle. Wash then rode out of the carnage and was fortunate enough to reach safety, even though his horse was again shot up. Dismounting the dying animal, he walked over to check on Private Henry McCollister. McCollister was wounded in the shoulder, and had five other bullet holes through his clothing. A Confederate tried to shoot Sergeant Elliott Norton in the face, but missed. Norton made it back unhurt and took charge of the survivors of Company B. Company F fared a little better. Lieutenant George Crawford, then in temporary command of the company, was wounded and lost a leg. His brother Francis was captured. Five men were killed, and ten others wounded in the action. In contrast, Lieutenant-Colonel Shepard reported one man killed and seven wounded from his entire Brigade.[16]

First Sergeant George Patten

Photo courtesy of Richard Hamilton.

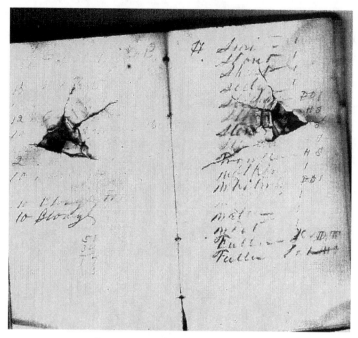

George Patten's Notebook with a bullet hole.
Courtesy of Richard Hamilton.

"Gallant charge by two companies of the 6th Michigan on Tuesday morning on the rebel rearguard, near
Falling Waters, where part of the rebel army crossed the Potomac"
Drawing by Edwin Forbes
Library of Congress

Company B's seven men were grouped with the survivors of Company F, now under the command of First Lieutenant Don Lovell. Though severely reduced in number, the squadron still had its duty to do. The war went on, and the pursuit of Lee and his Army continued. On July 17, three days after Falling Waters, the Michigan Cavalry Brigade crossed the Potomac into Virginia. For the men of the Squadron, the next seven days were a blurred, numbing mix of marches, standing "To horse" in rainstorms through the night, little sleep or decent food, and the prospect of battle with a still dangerous enemy.[17]

General Custer assumed command of the division on the day after Falling Waters, and the Michigan Brigade was temporarily under Colonel George Gray of the Sixth Michigan. On July 24, contact was made with the rebels at Battle Mountain near Newby's Cross-Roads. Custer attacked and engaged Confederate Infantry of Lieutenant-General A.P. Hill's Third Corps. During the fighting, two Rebel Brigades moved around the left flank and trapped the Fifth and Sixth Michigan Regiments and a two gun section of artillery. Colonel Gray and his wolverines fought hard to get themselves out of the trap. During the fight, Corporal Allen Pease and Private Lewis Bowman of Company B were riding side-by-side on a country lane when an enemy volley killed Bowman, and Pease's horse. With Bowman's death, Pease became one of six still living who came out of the charge at Falling Waters unscathed. He had another close call when a bullet went through his uniform at the shoulder as he sought cover. Continued Rebel fire forced him to leave his extra clothing and personal possessions on his dead horse and move deep into some woods. Left behind with five others on foot, they managed to escape a few hours later with the help of two slaves.[18]

After Battle Mountain, the Brigade was sent to Amissville where the men enjoyed a few days of rest, regular meals, and a comfortable camp. This was a well deserved and much needed break, the like of which they had not enjoyed since leaving their camps near Fairfax, Virginia at the beginning of the campaign. From Amissville, the Brigade was ordered to Warrenton Junction. By early August, camps were set up and the men settled into them. Expeditions were sent South across the Rappahannock to scout the Confederate Army, and North to hunt for Mosby and his partisans. What was left of Company B saw little service except picket duty until their numbers increased. Some men were recalled from details, and others who lost their horses and had gone to get remounts returned, which brought their number up to fifteen. It was a time for healing and recovery.[19]

NOTES

1   Kidd, 161, 163, 165-167.

2   ibid, 168-171; Haven, 33-35.

3   RSMV-36, 138; Civil War Compiled Military Service Record for Nelson Thomas (POW record and muster rolls), Records of the Adjutant General's Office, Record Group 94, National Archives, Washington, D.C.

4   Kidd, 171-172.

5   ibid, 172-174; Haven, 33.

6   Kidd, 174-178; Haven 33; Robertson, 581; Robert Underwood and Clarence Buel, eds., *Battles and Leaders of the Civil War*, 4 Vols. (New York: The Century Co., 1888), Vol. 3, 426-427 (Imboden's Account). Hereafter cited as B&L.

7   Kidd, 178-181; Robertson, 581.

8   Kidd, 178, 181; Haven, 34.

9   Kidd, 181-183; Robertson, 581.

10   Kidd, 184-185; Haven, 35; Robertson, 581, 584-585.

11   Kidd, 185-186; Haven, 35; Robertson, 585.

12   OR, Series I, Vol. 27, Pt. 2, 637-640 (Heth's report).

13   Kidd, 186; Haven, 35; Robertson, 581, 584-585; OR, 990 (Kilpatrick's report), 1000 (Custer's report), Pt. 2, 640-641 (Heth's report), 648 (Shepard's report).

14   Kidd, 187-190; Haven, 35; Robertson, 581,585; OR, 989-990 (Kilpatrick's Report), Pt. 2, 641 (Heth's report), 648 (Shepard's report).

15   RSMV-36, 20, 24, 30, 36, 60, 62, 81, 85, 88, 91, 93, 99, 106, 107, 110, 118, 119, 126, 146; Elliott M. Norton to Daniel H. Powers, August 2, 1863, Diary and Correspondence in possession of David Van Dyke, Nappanee, Indiana.

16   Pension Application File for Henry H. McCollister, SC-538774 (Statement by Henry Stewart), Records of the Veterans Administration, Record Group 15, National Archives, Washington, D.C.; Daniel Stewart to Lucretia Stewart, August 6, 1863, Regional History Collections, File A-284, East Bldg., East Campus, Western Michigan University, Kalamazoo, Michigan; Norton to Powers, August 2, 1863; OR, Pt. 2, 648 (Shepard's report); *New York Times,* July 29, 1863, Casualty Lists.

17   Norton to Powers, August 2, 1863; OR, Pt.1, 1000-1001 (Custer's report).

18   RSMV-36, 25; Haven, 40-41.

19   Haven, 41; Norton to Powers, August 2, 1863; OR, 1004 (Custer's report).

GETTYSBURG'S AFTERMATH

Company B started in Grand Rapids with ninety-nine officers and men. By August 1, 1863, after ten months and one campaign, it was down to fifteen men. The rest were already discharged for disability, on detail, in hospitals sick or wounded, in a parole camp, prisoners of war, or dead. Commissary Sergeant Pliny Smith showed up and tried to get command of the company, and with it, a commission. Up to that time, Smith had not been with the unit at the front, and the men had no respect for him. Lieutenant Lovell told Sergeant Norton to ignore Smith and take care of his men. With his ambitions thwarted, Smith used his position as Commissary Sergeant to make life as difficult as he could for the men.[1]

Company B's contingent in the Westchester parole camp had their own set of problems. Lieutenant Powers was placed in command of one hundred cavalry troopers, which included his own men. He was responsible for drilling them and assigning work details. The only differences between them and soldiers with the army were they could not be armed or leave the camp. Hygiene was a major concern, as most of the men were infested with body lice. A constant problem for soldiers in the field, this was a particularly acute case. The men had lost everything but the clothes they wore when they were captured.

61

When they washed what was left of their uniforms, they had to stand naked until the rags dried.[2]

Powers and his men were in the parole camp for about six weeks when the paroles of the enlisted men were declared illegal. In July of 1862, Major General John Dix of the United States Army, and Major General Daniel H. Hill of the Confederate States Army, agreed to a set of articles, a cartel, for paroling prisoners of war. Article seven stated that prisoners could be paroled on the field if both opposing army commanders agreed. On July 4, General Lee sent a note to General Meade proposing an exchange. Meade refused. With no agreement, prisoners for both sides had to be taken to pre-arranged release points to be paroled. In the case of Stuart's prisoners, he should have taken them to the release point, but instead paroled them where he was, merely to free himself of the responsibility. Citing article seven of the cartel, those federal soldiers paroled by Stuart at Dover were sent back to their units in the third week of August, including the fourteen men from Company B. Lieutenant Powers remained on parole, awaiting exchange due to his being an officer, but he was released from the parole camp and authorized a short leave.[3]

Private Oscar Stout was the lone exception from the group of parolees. At the first opportunity, Stout made his way back to his wife Elizabeth, in Courtland Township, Kent County, Michigan. He stayed for over three months, and helped on the farm during harvest. He probably reasoned if he had to sit out of the war for a time, he might as well spend it at home being useful, rather than marking time in a parole camp in Pennsylvania. Reluctantly, Oscar turned himself in to military authorities at Detroit on October 16, and rejoined the company in early November. Initially charged with desertion, he never faced a court-martial, and the charge was later dropped.[4]

Back in Grand Rapids, there were celebrations for the victories at Gettysburg and Vicksburg. There were also the funerals and services for the dead, which counted the cost of such victories.

Immediately after the battle at Falling Waters, Lieutenant-Colonel Thaddeus Foote and three soldiers recovered the bodies of Weber and Captain Royce. Lieutenant Bolza and the enlisted men were temporarily buried near the battle site. Lieutenant Elliot Covell of the Fifth Michigan was assigned to take Weber and Royce home. Covell took them to Harper's Ferry where they were embalmed and put in metal coffins. He then put them on a train and took them back to Michigan.[5]

On Friday, July 24, just ten days after the battle, Weber's body arrived in Grand Rapids. As it was the custom then, Weber's coffin was kept at the family home overnight. Due to Weber having been killed by a shot through his head, the flag-draped coffin remained closed. Next day, his widowed mother and two sisters led a procession of his many friends and admirers to St. Marks Episcopal Church. After the funeral service, which was attended by Colonel Alger of the Fifth Michigan and Captain Thompson of Company A of the Sixth, who were home convalescing from wounds, mourners resumed the slow march in carriages to Fulton Street Cemetery. Here the Masons conducted graveside services for their fallen brother.[6]

**MONUMENT FOR PETER A. WEBER
FULTON STREET CEMETERY, GRAND RAPIDS, MICHIGAN**

**HEADSTONE FOR FRANCIS W. KELLOGG
IS ONE OF THE SMALL MARKERS IN LINE BEHIND IT**

Lieutenant Bolza's body remained in Maryland. Orphaned at an early age, he had no other family. In 1856 he had come to Grand Rapids from New York, and later purchased part of a jewelry business from the father of Sergeant Edmund Dikeman. His remains now rest in Antietam National Battlefield Cemetery.[7]

CHARLES E. BOLZA
PRE-WAR PHOTO

Photo courtesy of the Grand Rapids History & Special Collections,
Archives, Grand Rapids Public Library, Grand Rapids, Michigan

Sutler Lyman Patten and his brother Charles, Sixth Michigan's Regimental Quartermaster, returned to the battle site later in the year and retrieved the body of their cousin, First Sergeant George Patten. Transported back home, he was laid to rest in the family plot of Brooklawn Cemetery in Walker Township, Kent County, Michigan. Sadly, Patten's father Lyman died of a stroke on Christmas Eve of that same year, leaving his mother Sarah to raise her grandson alone.[8]

Like everywhere across the country, both North and South, losses like these were felt by everyone in the area. Civic, church, and business activities connected nearly everyone in the city and surrounding communities. Everyone knew nearly everyone else, or knew of them. Weber's house was just a half-block from the home of Charles Patten, and Daniel Powers and his family knew Lyman Patten very well before the war. Allen Pease's Father-in-Law and Harvey Smith had worked for the Withey family, Colonel Gray's former law partner, and Pease himself rented from the Dikeman's. It was a smaller world then.[9]

Chaplain Stephen Greeley was home recovering from illness after the Gettysburg campaign. James Kidd's description of Greeley explained why. "He was a powerful pulpit orator. A kind-hearted, simple minded gentleman of the old school, not at all fitted for the hardships and exposure that he had to undergo while following the fortunes of General Custer's troopers in Virginia. Army life was too much for him to endure, and it was as much as he could do to look after his own physical well-being, and the spiritual condition of his flock was apt to be sadly neglected. He stayed with the regiment till the end but, in the field he was more like a child than a seasoned soldier and needed the watchful care of all his friends to keep him from perishing with hunger, fatigue, and exposure. I always forgot my own discomforts in commiseration of those of the honest chaplain."[10]

On August 10, trustees of the First Congregational Church announced that Greeley had until October 1 to resign his position with the Sixth Michigan Cavalry and return to his pulpit labors in Grand Rapids. He had tendered his resignation from the Army earlier in the year, but had been refused. Accepting the decision of commanders to keep him, he did not shrink from any of his responsibilities to the troopers of the Sixth. Twelve days later, with his health restored, he said goodbye to his wife and two children, and boarded a train bound for Washington, D.C.[11]

Company B of the Sixth Michigan Cavalry Regiment was a rare unit in the Civil War. After its first year in existence, and its first campaign, it had suffered more battle casualties (38) than losses from disease and disability (24). Eight men had transferred to other companies within the regiment. Private Monroe was transferred to the Invalid Corps, soon to be known as the Veteran Reserve Corps, on July 1. Private William Green died of disease in Washington on August 17. In September, Private Howe was discharged disabled. Corporal O'Dell and Private Rust were permanently lost to the company later in the year, but were in the hospital during the campaign. Charles Watkins was discharged to accept a commission in the Tenth Michigan Cavalry being organized in Grand Rapids. Whatever the reasons were, Company B's numbers, and combat effectiveness, were severely reduced.[12]

Having performed well at Hanover and Gettysburg, and during the pursuit of Lee's army to the Potomac River, the company was nearly destroyed at Falling Waters. They were ordinary men, who had experienced extraordinary events. Some died, but all those who survived came away with an altered outlook on life, and gave much more thought to what they were risking their lives to accomplish.

NOTES

1   Norton to Powers, August 2, 1863.

2   Haven, 33, 34; Daniel H. Powers to his parents, July 19, 1863.

3   Haven, 42, 43, 45; *Grand Rapids Daily Eagle*, October 29, 1863, 1; OR, Series II, Vol. 4, 265-268 (The cartel); OR, Series I, Vol. 27, Pt. 1, 78 (Meade's report); OR, Series I, Vol. 27, Pt. 3, 514 (Notes between Lee and Meade); OR, Series II, Vol. 6, 78-79, 199 (War Dept. General Orders #207 ordering release of prisoners and reasons for order).

4   Civil War Combined Military Service Record for Oscar Stout, and notations in morning reports for Company B, 6th Michigan Cavalry, Records of the Adjutant General's Office, Record Group 94, National Archives, Washington, D.C.

5   *Grand Rapids Daily Eagle,* July 25, 1863, 2.

6   *Detroit Advertiser and Tribune,* July 28, 1863, 2; *Grand Rapids Daily Eagle,* July 27, 1863, 1.

7   *Grand Rapids Daily Eagle,* 26 July 1863, 2; *1860 Grand Rapids City Directory,* Advertising Section and Individual Listings, 42; Antietam National Cemetery, Section 23, Lot A, Grave 32, Site 883, Author's Visit – Summer 2005.

8   Hamilton, 189, 190; Headstone Inscriptions from the Patten Family Plot, Brooklawn Cemetery, Walker Township, Kent County, Michigan, Author's visit, Summer 2000.

9   *1860 Grand Rapids City Directory,* 87, 108; Powers to his Parents, April 9, 1863; Haven, 16, 23.

10   Kidd, 55-56.

11   *Grand Rapids Daily Eagle,* July 20, 1863, 1; August 10, 1863, 1; August 22, 1863, 1.

12   RSMV-36 (Compiled statistics); RSMV-40, 145; Norton to Powers, August 2, 1863.

WINTER IN VIRGINIA

By the beginning of September, Company B had partially recovered from the effects of the Gettysburg campaign. With the men from parole camp plus those recalled from details back in the company, their numbers were brought to about twenty-five troopers - still far below its original and authorized strength.

Men became weary of the campaign trail, yet not willing to concede anything to their enemy. Wash Stewart expressed the attitude of most of those remaining in a letter to his cousin dated September 10. He wrote, "I have seen enough (fighting) for one year…You may think that I am sick of it, but that is not my name, for when I do a thing, I mean to stick to it…I am not spoiling for a fight, but if it has got to be done, I will try to do my share."[1]

Lieutenant Powers returned from leave and was promoted to Captain unofficially, but couldn't take command of the company until he was exchanged, so he was made acting Regimental Adjutant in the interim. While holding that office, Powers witnessed the battle of Culpepper. General Robert E. Lee had sent two divisions under Lieutenant General James Longstreet to help the Confederate Army defending Georgia and eastern Tennessee. Major-General George G. Meade learned of it, and took the opportunity to advance the Army of the Potomac to the Rapidan River. A cavalry fight took place at Culpepper, Virginia on September 13, but the Sixth Michigan was in a supporting role and took no part in it.[2]

Later in September, Meade was also asked to reinforce the western army and sent XI and XII Corps. When Lee discovered this, he countered by mounting his own offensive in early October. On the 11th, the Michigan Cavalry Brigade was pressed hard while withdrawing through Brandy Station to the Rappahannock River. A rear guard action under First-Lieutenant Don Lovell was skillfully executed, and allowed the Sixth to pull back safely. Company B was probably with Lovell, and suffered no casualties.[3]

Confederate forces advanced to near Bull Run while the Federal Army managed to stay between them and Washington. After his drive was stopped at Bristoe Station, Lee began to withdraw his troops back to the Rappahannock where his lines would be more secure. Meade naturally followed. Scouting to Gainesville, Sixth Michigan troopers reported enemy cavalry there in strength. As part of an operation involving the entire Third Cavalry Division, the Michigan Cavalry Brigade was ordered to scout across Broad Run, engage the rebels, and confirm Lee's withdrawal.

Pushing against relatively light resistance, the brigade reached Buckland Mills on October 19, and drove across Broad Run, halting about a mile beyond. Just as the men were tending their horses and preparing an overdue meal, the enemy suddenly attacked with both mounted and dismounted cavalry, supported by artillery. Jeb Stuart was attempting to trap Kilpatrick's command between Hampton's and Fitz Lee's Cavalry Divisions. A portion of Pennington's Battery came up and helped the Sixth Michigan, deployed as skirmishers, to hold back the rebels while Custer organized a brigade defense. After desperate fighting, Michigan troopers were pushed back on both flanks and forced to retire, in many cases with great haste and panic, back over Broad Run. It was a rout – worse than anything they had known before. Custer lost his headquarters wagon and personal papers in the confusion that followed. First Brigade, having been farther south of Broad Run, suffered a worse experience. In successfully covering his army's retrograde movement, Jeb Stuart caused an embarrassing episode for the federal cavalry which became known as the "Buckland Races."[4]

Before Buckland Mills, on September 30, Egbert Conklin had been made First Sergeant, filling the vacancy created when George Patten was killed. On the same day, Corporal James Johnson was promoted to Sergeant, and he became acting Quartermaster Sergeant while Nelson Thomas recovered from his wounds. Sergeant William Keyes returned to the company in late September after being wounded at Falling Waters, but his wounds were not healed well enough for him to participate in active operations, so he was made acting regimental Sergeant-Major to replace Henry Hobart, who was captured at Brandy station on October 11. Captain James Kidd had returned to the Sixth on October 12, after recovering from his wound received at Falling Waters. On November 1, he was promoted to Major, retroactive to May 9, and assumed field command of the regiment. In Company B, Privates John Newton, Wash Stewart, and Stephen Stowe were made Corporals. Corporal David McVean was advanced to Sergeant. Acting Captain Daniel Powers, although sick much of the time, resumed command. Due to their reduced numbers, most of the men were armed with Spencer repeating rifles. Those that weren't had Burnside breechloaders. Both weapons were much faster to fire than the Enfield rifles many of the rebels were armed with. Company B had structure and substance once again.[5]

Henry Washington Stewart

*Image provided by Garry
Bush*

**STEPHEN L. STOWE
PRE-WAR PHOTO**

Photo reproduced from a locket by Linda Longcore

Late in November, General Meade was ordered by President Lincoln to launch an attack before winter set in. The Michigan Brigade pushed across the Rappahannock and on to Stevensburg, where they met heavy resistance from Wade Hampton's cavalry, covering the Confederate Army's retreat beyond the Rapidan River. On November 26, when the Mine Run offensive began, there was a fight at Morton's Ford, but it had little influence on the operation. By early December, both

DAVID E. McVEAN
QUARTERMASTER SERGEANT

Photo Courtesy of the State Archives of Michigan

armies were settling into winter camps. The Michigan Brigade was headquartered at Stevensburg, from which the men pulled picket duty along the Rapidan. Guard, drill, and work details were the camp routine for the Michigan cavalrymen during the winter of 1863-1864. It was dull and seemingly endless, but at that time, preferred to fighting.[6]

With the seasonal lull in active operations came an opportunity to address problems that could not be solved while on campaign. Damaged or lost equipment and weapons were replaced, new clothing issued, and horses that had managed to survive the recent battles were examined, and if necessary, exchanged. The quality of horses the men rode was a constant concern. Some of the mounts received at the remount station were as bad, or worse, than those being replaced. When a complaint was made by Custer, Major General George Stoneman, then Chief of the Cavalry Bureau for the U.S. Army, characterized the Wolverines as being "great horse killers," and dismissed the objection. As an example that both sides of the argument could claim – the horse belonging to William Whitney of Company B gave out and died while on routine picket duty.[7]

Replacements were necessary to bring the company back up to a respectable fighting strength. For that purpose, First-Sergeant Egbert Conklin was sent home to Grand Rapids on recruiting duty. Conklin conducted a recruiting campaign that drew men from communities throughout western Michigan. In addition to this effort, a platoon of men primarily from Lenawee, Hillsdale, and Jackson counties in eastern Michigan was enlisted. Many of the men came from or signed up in Woodstock Township in northwestern Lenawee County. From this group, Charles Parker of Addison was commissioned a Second Lieutenant.[8]

Men enlisted from western Michigan were:
Arsnoe, Augustus
Arsnoe, James
Blood, Abel
Fields, George
Hoskins, Madison
McCollum, George
Milton, John
Moss, George
Perry, Arthur

Reynolds, William
Schofield, Edgar
Underhill, Charles
Vose, Samuel
Winkworth, Robert
    Men enlisted from eastern Michigan were:
Baker, Asa
Beaman, Joshua,
Bodely, Thomas
Burder, John
Doty, Henry
Elmore, Byron
English, Martin
Goucher, Charles
Goucher, Homer
Jones, James
Jones, Robert
McCall, Donald
McLarren, Andrew
Moore, Richard
Onweller, William
Post, Charles
Randall, George
Smith, Jacob
Swain, Sardius
Swarthout, John
Tillapaw, Lafayette
Turner, Byron
Turner, James
Vanetten, Jacob
Walter, William
    Most of the men were enlisted in December 1863 or January 1864, and a few in February. Lieutenant Parker's commission

was dated February 3, and he was mustered into federal service on the 16th. Matthew Kettle had enlisted in August, and George Labell in October 1863, and were already with the unit. Winkworth was almost immediately transferred to Company F.

George Moss was the younger brother of William Moss, an original member of the company. George had been with the unit for some time prior to his enlistment, being employed to attend the baggage and belongings of the officers. Without any officers in the company after July 14, there wasn't much for him to do except wait for Lieutenant Powers to return. He was liked and accepted by the men, and his situation was an additional sore point between them and Commissary Sergeant Pliny Smith. George was not a soldier, but merely a civilian employee of the officers, so Smith refused to allow him rations or draw any clothing. The men shared their rations and clothing with George, despite Smith's objections. Moss probably went home with Conklin in December, to spend time with family prior to his enlistment. On January 15, 1864, Private Perley Johnson, who had been detailed to the Commissary Department for the past year, was promoted to Commissary Sergeant, and Pliny Smith took Johnson's place on the detail.[9]

Recruits from western Michigan rendezvoused in early January at Camp Kellogg/Lee in Grand Rapids, where they were mustered into federal service and may have received some basic military instruction. Lieutenant Parker's contingent may have gathered at Grand Rapids, Jackson, or some other location, but they were also sworn in at that time. By early February they were put on a train to join their unit. Most of the men reported to Acting Captain Powers at Stevensburg, Virginia on February 13 and 18. Some became so sick on the trip they went straight to a hospital when they reached Washington or Stevensburg. Private Charles Goucher died of disease on February 23, shortly after he arrived. Homer Goucher, younger brother of Charles, Charles Mead, who was originally enlisted for D Company, and George McCollum, reported in March.[10]

As soon as the recruits were settled in camp they were issued horses, arms, and equipment. Then drill began – for everyone. The single rank method of maneuver learned from General Cooke's manual was set aside for the double rank method Dragoons of the pre-war army used. This meant the "old" men drilled alongside the recruits, which helped to meld the two groups into one, smoothly operating unit. Combat experience was the difference between them, and that would soon be remedied.[11]

Another change was the armament of the regiment. The Spencer rifles were exchanged throughout the time they spent in winter camp for the shorter carbine model, which allowed troopers to fight more easily while mounted. There were still some Burnside carbines in the Sixth, and the First Michigan kept some Sharp's carbines they had originally been armed with. Fifth Michigan had Spencer rifles issued to them when they got to Washington, and Seventh Michigan was issued only a few shoulder fired weapons when they first arrived, but now all the regiments were similarly armed. General Custer would normally use the First and Seventh regiments as saber units – fighting mounted, while the Fifth and Sixth regiments fought dismounted because of the Spencer rifles. Although this method was generally continued, any regiment in the brigade was now capable of operating either way.[12]

In February, Brigadier General Judson Kilpatrick, assisted by Colonel Ulric Dahlgren, formed a plan to raid Richmond and free union prisoners held there. The plan was approved by President Lincoln and Major General Henry Halleck, General-in-Chief of the U.S. Army. Volunteers were taken from the veterans of the Michigan Brigade, with Major James Kidd commanding the contingent from the Sixth. General Custer was given temporary command of other troops and ordered to create a diversion in the direction of Gordonsville. On the night of February 28, the raid began. Riding for two days, the command approached to within five miles of Richmond, where they were held up by enemy artillery and a local defense force. Fearing Confederate reinforcements, Kilpatrick decided to fall back to Mechanicsville, where his force was attacked that night. With the Sixth as part of the rear guard, he led his column into federal positions on the peninsula along the James River and ended the raid. Described as a dismal failure, rumors that one of the raid's objectives was to assassinate Confederate leaders made it an embarrassment as well. Participants were put aboard vessels and brought to Alexandria. After debarking, they marched back to Stevensburg.[13]

Upon their return, there was another round of promotions. With Second Lieutenant Parker reporting for duty, Nelson Thomas was elevated to First Lieutenant on March 14. Two days later, James Johnson, recently returned from leave in Michigan, became Quartermaster Sergeant. On the same day, Ezra Brown was promoted to Corporal, and Corporal Stephen Stowe was made a Sergeant. Edmund Dikeman was also promoted to Sergeant after having been reduced to Private in November. In contrast, for reasons unknown, Edwin Whitney requested to be demoted to Private. Fortunately, he changed his mind and was promoted to Sergeant two months later, when Dikeman was again reduced. Daniel Powers mustered in as Captain on March 17, retroactive to Weber's death at Falling Waters. Three days later, Solon Bentley made Corporal.[14]

Command changes were made at higher levels as well. U.S. Grant was promoted to Lieutenant General and made commander of the entire United States Army. His headquarters was in the field with the Army of the Potomac, which remained under Major General George Meade's command. Cavalry

Federal Cavalry Raids

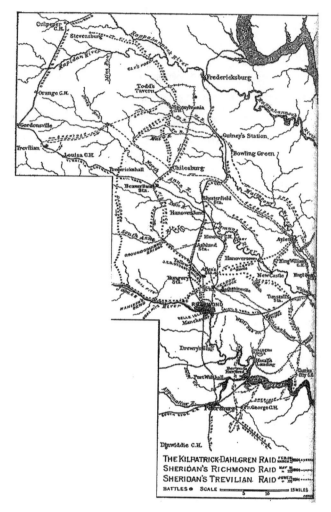

From Battles and Leaders of the Civil War, Ed. Robert
Underwood and Clarence Buel

Corps Chief Alfred Pleasonton was replaced by Major General
Philip Sheridan, a former commander of the Second Michigan
Cavalry. After the raid on Richmond, Judson Kilpatrick, or "Kill
Cavalry," as he was aptly nicknamed, was sent west and James

80

Wilson took command of the Third Cavalry Division. This did not concern the Wolverines much, as Custer and his Michigan Cavalry Brigade became First Brigade, First Cavalry Division under the leadership of Brigadier General Alfred Torbert.[15]

Colonel Gray had been battling a drinking problem and the resultant health issues, and was sitting on a permanent court-martial board in Washington. Under pressure from some quarters in Michigan, and not wanting to hold the Colonelcy when he was unable to serve in the field with the regiment, he resigned his commission on May 19. Major James Kidd became the official commander of the Sixth Michigan Cavalry, as well as leading it in the field.[16]

Companies I and M returned to the regiment from more than a year of detached duty in the Shenandoah Valley. The Sixth Michigan Cavalry was complete again. Drills and picket duty continued through April and into May. Rain fell much of the time. As the weather became warmer, everyone knew they would soon be on the campaign trail again. Boredom and monotony would be replaced by the chance of agonizing death or mutilation. Men took the possibilities in stride, with a determination to see the war through to the end. With that goal in their minds, they broke camp on May 4, and marched south.[17]

NOTES

1 Henry W. Stewart to "Cousin M", September 10, 1863, Regional History Collections, File #A-284, East Bldg., East Campus, Western Michigan University, Kalamazoo, Michigan.

2 Daniel Powers to Jonathan Powers Sr., September 17, 1863; *Grand Rapids Daily Eagle*, October 29, 1863, 1.

3 Kidd, 208-209; OR, Series I, Vol. 29, Pt. 1, 390-391 (Custer's report).

4   Kidd, 213-226; Robertson, 589-591; OR, 389-392 (Custer's report); 438-439, 451-452 (Stuart's report); 464 (Fitz Lee's report).

5   RSMV-36, 36, 81, 90, 100, 133, 135; Civil War Compiled Military Service Records for each of the individuals plus notes in the records of Elliott Norton; Daniel H. Powers to Jonathan Powers Sr., September 17, 1863.

6   Kidd, 227-229.

7   Order Book for Company B, Clothing issues, 6ᵗʰ Michigan Cavalry Regimental Records, Record Group 94, National Archives, Washington, D.C.; OR, Series I, Vol. 29, Pt. 2, 448-449 (Custer letter dated November 12, 1863, Pleasonton's endorsement, and Stoneman's response); Diary entry for Daniel H. Powers, February 26, 1864.

8   Civil War Military Service Record for Egbert Conklin (Notes on muster rolls from Dec. 1863 through April 1864), Record Group 94, National Archives, Washington, D.C.; RSMV-36.

9   Elliott Norton to Daniel Powers, August 2, 1863; RSMV-36, 77.

10   Diary entries for Daniel Powers, February 13 and 18, 1864; Notes on Morning Reports for Feb. and Mar. 1864, Records of the Adjutant General's Office, Record Group 94, National Archives, Washington, D.C.; RSMV-36, 60.

11   Kidd, 232-233; Diary entry for Frank Gross, March 30, 1864, Bentley Historical Library, University of Michigan, Ann Arbor, Michigan.

12   Kidd, 78, 255.

13   ibid, 234-260; Haven, 58-59; B&L, Vol. 4, 93-96, 190; OR, Series I, Vol. 33, 161-166, 181-188; Diary entry for Frank Gross, March 19, 1864.

14   RSMV-36, 22, 27, 46, 77, 111, 135, 138; Military Service Record for Edwin E. Whitney, notation on Muster Rolls for March through June 1864.

15   Kidd, 261-262.

16   RSMV-36, 61.

17   Kidd, 264; Diary entry for Frank Gross, May 5, 1864.

ACROSS THE RAPIDAN

General Grant began his offensive operations on May 4, but there was little activity for the cavalrymen from Michigan. After the first day's march, they went into night camp only four miles from their starting point, having been assigned to protect the rear of the army and help prevent straggling. Next day, the march was continued across the Rapidan River and into an area of Virginia known as the Wilderness – to a place behind the left flank of the army. At an extremely early hour on May 6, the Brigade was back in the saddle and riding for Brock road. Arriving in pre-dawn darkness, the Sixth was placed in line behind the First Michigan, facing an opening in the woods, on the right flank. Men were told to stand by their horses and wait for orders. Two companies, one from the First and one from the Sixth, were out front as pickets.[1]

With first light came the opening shots. Confederate cavalry, commanded by Brigadier General Thomas Rosser, a former West Point classmate of Custer, pushed the pickets back to the main lines of federal horsemen, who were by then mounted and ready. Custer ordered the charge, and formations of blue uniformed cavalry surged out into the clearing. A ditch prevented a full impact of the opposing forces, yet a brisk fight developed. Rebel artillery was brought up to help break the union line. Custer thought there was danger on the right flank

83

and ordered the Sixth there, with additional instructions to silence the enemy cannon.[2]

The Sixth was scattered due to the charge, but Major Kidd gathered as many men as he could and sidestepped behind the First and into position. Troopers left their horses and were moving up to attack when they encountered dismounted Confederate cavalry. Rosser and Custer had the same idea. Rebel lines overlapped the Sixth's, so Kidd had the right flank refused to a ninety degree angle.[3]

Battle lines were pressed hard by the enemy, and for a moment it appeared they might push the Sixth back and endanger the entire Brigade. Before being forced to give ground, the Fifth Michigan arrived, and together the two regiments swept forward and slowly drove the enemy back. Company B's only casualty in this fight was Private Frank Gross, who was severely wounded.[4]

After the enemy broke away, the Michigan Brigade was ordered back to the rear of the army to protect supply trains. Next day was occupied by retaking ground given up the previous evening. Assigned a supporting role, the Sixth was again withdrawn to the rear for the night. May 8 was spent trying to march, and getting into traffic jams with the infantry. During that time, Generals Sheridan and Meade had a confrontation over the performance of the cavalry, which resulted in Meade allowing Sheridan, with General Grant's approval, to lead a raid toward Richmond. Devised to draw Jeb Stuart and his Confederate cavalry into a major battle, Sheridan's plan was to completely destroy them.[5]

Three divisions of U.S. cavalry marched before dawn on May 9, with the Michigan Brigade leading the corps, and the Sixth leading the brigade. A pace was set so that horses and men would not be exhausted before they met the enemy – a pleasant change from previous raids. Marching past the right flank of the rebel army, the federal cavalry rode on in the direction of Richmond.[6]

As the column approached the Virginia Central Railroad, a battalion of the First Michigan was sent ahead, and came upon a group of Yankee prisoners being marched to waiting trains for transport to prison camps in the South. Sweeping in, the First released the prisoners, and took some of their former guards captive. As this action ended, the Sixth Michigan moved up and joined the First. Together, the two units charged into Beaver Dam Station and captured the town, two trains, and a large amount of supplies intended for Lee's army. What the men couldn't carry away they destroyed, then returned to the column and continued the march.[7]

On the morning of May 11, Sheridan was brought to battle by Stuart, who had two brigades of dismounted cavalry and two batteries of artillery near a place called Yellow Tavern. A sharp skirmish was in progress when the Michigan Brigade reached the battlefield. Troops were in columns, and remained in the saddle on the side of the road behind the lines. General Sheridan approached, and Major Kidd announced him to the men, who respectfully cheered. For most of them, it was a first look at their new Corps Commander. Sheridan was a West Point graduate, small in stature, with a fiery Irish temper, yet steady and decisive. These were traits that would serve the federal forces well in the coming months. After acknowledging their salute, Sheridan rode on to the front.[8]

A short time later, an order was given for the Fifth and Sixth Michigan to dismount and form line-of-battle, with the Sixth on the right. Troopers of the two regiments moved forward to a fence, beyond which was a field. While halted at the fence, enemy fire was received from the woods on the opposite side of the field. A staff officer had approached Major Kidd and took his attention away from the fight for a moment, when the Fifth suddenly climbed over the fence and charged across the field. Not wanting to be left behind, the Sixth jumped up and, without orders, charged as well, leaving their commander in their wake. Kidd and the staff officer agreed there was no stopping them. Recovering quickly, Kidd followed his men across the field wondering who was leading whom in his regiment.[9]

Federal Cavalry Raids

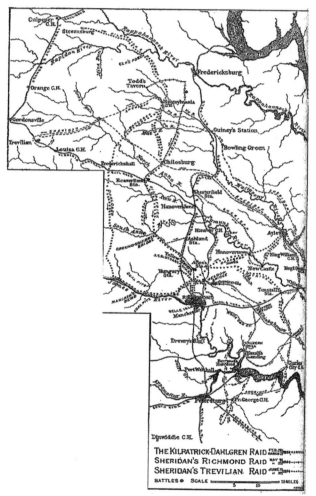

From Battles and Leaders of the Civil War, Ed. Robert
Underwood and Clarence Buel

After clearing the woods of enemy soldiers, the line was reformed with the Sixth on the left. The Confederates had retreated to a second position on the crest of a ridge. Between that ridge and the woods, occupied by Michigan troopers, was another large field, with a fence and tree line on the far side.[10]

A section of rebel artillery fired into the woods held by the Fifth and Sixth, but did little damage. The real danger came from sharpshooters in the tree line in front of them. A wave of Michigan troopers again swept across the field and cleared the tree line. Pushing on under heavy fire, the men reached the shelter of a ditch near the base of the ridge. After a prolonged firefight, Sheridan ordered Custer to charge the enemy guns and take the ridge. While the Sixth and Fifth moved forward once again on foot, the rest of the brigade made a mounted charge. Throwing themselves upon a stubborn adversary, the Wolverines finally convinced the enemy to relinquish the ridge and end the fighting. Moving off the battlefield, the column reformed and continued the march. Several days later the Michigan Brigade learned Confederate General J.E.B. Stuart had been mortally wounded in the final stages of that battle.[11]

On the morning of May 12, the brigade was ordered to take the Meadow bridges over the Chickahominy River. When they arrived they found the main bridge partially destroyed, but the railroad bridge was intact. On the opposite side of the span was a patch of woods occupied by rebel skirmishers. Beyond the trees was a line of breastworks supported by artillery. Custer ordered the Fifth and Sixth to dismount, cross the bridge, and seize the woods. Although it was slow and hazardous work, the men made their way over the spaced planks of the structure, formed into line, and cleared the woods of Confederates. Troopers then halted at the edge of the woods and engaged in a firefight with enemy soldiers behind the breastworks. That part of the battle lasted two to three hours, and allowed time for the main bridge to be rebuilt. Second and Third Brigades of the First Cavalry Division then crossed the river and helped push the enemy out of the breastworks. Second and Third Divisions, which had also been fighting that morning, made their way to the rebuilt bridge. The entire Cavalry Corps spent that night at Gaines Mill. During the fighting in the woods, Private Sardius Swain, one of the new men, and Corporal John Newton, of Company B, were wounded.[12]

At dawn, the corps marched on with no more trouble from the rebels. As the column approached the James River, a few rounds were fired at them by their own gunboats. It was soon stopped and the men went into camp at Malvern Hill, fairly pleased that nobody was shooting at them – friend or foe. After three days of rest and resupply, the federal horsemen continued their march back to the Army of the Potomac. On May 19, third day of the march from the James, the Sixth was sent to destroy Bottom's Bridge. Next day the column was approaching Hanover Court House when scouts encountered resistance. Major Kidd and the Sixth were tasked to flank the enemy and secure the town, which they did with little difficulty, and no blood. Most of the enemy force had moved on and were pursued briefly by the rest of the brigade. Continuing on, the column crossed the Pamunkey River over a rebuilt bridge on May 22. Three days later, the cavalry rejoined the army and the raid ended.[13]

On May 26, the brigade was back on the Pamunkey to secure crossings at Hanovertown for the Army of the Potomac as it continued its drive toward Richmond. After crossing the river next morning, the Sixth was ordered to advance from Hanovertown toward Hanover Court House. After going about a mile, they were stopped by dismounted Confederate cavalry in positions hastily prepared in a patch of woods. First Michigan came up in support with the Sixth on the right. Both regiments attacked, hoping to break the rebel defense quickly. Frontal assault failed, but the First and Sixth held the enemy's attention while the Fifth and Seventh Michigan maneuvered around the flank. Forced to retreat, the rebels did not trouble the army as it crossed the river.[14]

Another cavalry division took the lead next day, and had proceeded to Haw's Shop when dismounted Confederate cavalry was again encountered in strong positions blocking the road. Fighting took place in a large patch of woods which the road passed through. Threatening to break the federal line, the rebels were pressing hard when the Michigan Brigade came up. Troopers left their horses and formed two ranks, with the Sixth on the right side of the road. Moving into the woods, they engaged the enemy – a big, new brigade from South Carolina. Experiencing combat for the first time, the South Carolinians fought well. Firearms of the combatants were the deciding factors. Michigan soldiers had Spencer repeating carbines, while most of the South Carolina troopers used single-shot Enfield rifles. Slowly the tide turned, and the rebels were forced to retire. Eighteen men from the Sixth were killed or mortally wounded at Haw's Shop. Private Byron Elmore, another of the new recruits for Company B, died on June 17 of wounds received that day.[15]

After tending to their casualties, the men mounted up and rode through the night. On May 30 and 31 the brigade was heavily engaged, but the Sixth was held in reserve and saw no action. At dawn on June 1, the federal cavalry was occupying breastworks defending a position at Cold Harbor. Pressured by enemy infantry, they held until relieved by VI Corps troops around noon. For the next four days, Sixth Michigan secured a river crossing site. On June 6, the Michigan Brigade camped at New Castle Ferry and prepared for its next mission.[16]

Another raid was conceived that would take the rebel cavalry away the Army of the Potomac's area of operations, and disrupt supplies going to the Army of Northern Virginia from the Shenandoah Valley by destroying a portion of the Virginia Central Railroad. First and Second Cavalry divisions were selected to carry out the raid.

Departing New Castle Ferry on the morning of June 7, the column marched North to Aylett's. From there the federal horsemen rode between the Mattapony and Pamunkey Rivers toward Chilesburg. Following the North Anna River, they crossed at Carpenter's Ford and turned to the Southwest. Foraging parties had instructions to "commandeer" food, horses, and other supplies from the farms and communities along the way. This was an established method of resupply on the move in enemy territory which both sides practiced.[17]

On the night of June 10, the Michigan Brigade was camped near Buck Chiles' farm. The rest of Sheridan's corps was just up the road near Clayton's store. They were only a few miles from their objective – Trevilian Station. Scrub brush and woods dominated the landscape, broken by large open fields primarily south of the railroad.[18]

In the early morning hours, Confederate cavalrymen from Fitzhugh Lee's Division probed the picket line of the Seventh Michigan on the road between the Chiles farm and Louisa Court House, then withdrew. At dawn Sheridan moved on Trevilian Station, but his path was blocked by dismounted Confederate cavalry, and a brisk fight developed.

Custer took his brigade down a backwoods lane on Sheridan's left flank, with the Fifth Michigan in the lead. As the Fifth emerged from the woods, they spotted supply trains, ambulances, and horses belonging to the dismounted rebels opposing Sheridan. Custer ordered the Fifth to charge and capture them. Down the road they went, to the station and beyond, trying to head off the lead wagons attempting to escape.[19]

Confederates heard the commotion behind them, and moved to protect their position. A part of the Seventh Georgia Cavalry appeared at the head of the column, cutting the Fifth Michigan off from the rest of the Brigade. Custer and his staff were in front trading shots with the enemy as the Sixth came out of the woods. Custer ordered Major Kidd to charge the rebels and drive them back. Kidd brought up a battalion commanded by Captain Harvey Vinton and led it in an attack on the Georgians. Some of the rebels fled, but others merely moved out of the way and then turned to attack the flank and rear of Vinton's battalion as it went by. Major Kidd was briefly made a prisoner until a second battalion, commanded by Captain Manning Birge, charged in and made it possible for Kidd to escape. As Birge continued on, he ran into a larger enemy force. He immediately turned his troops around and raced back to his starting point, pursued by those Confederates. As Birge reached the relative safety of the Sixth's lines, his pursuers were greeted by a volley from a third battalion commanded by Captain Don Lovell.[20]

After throwing the Confederates back, Custer moved his brigade toward Trevilian Station to support the Fifth Michigan. As he did so, he was confronted by his old friend Tom Rosser in front from the west, and Fitzhugh Lee's Division coming from Louisa Court House to the east, on his left and rear. Virtually surrounded in a field with very little cover, the Michigan Brigade stood its ground and fought hard to avoid disaster.

When Rosser attacked the Fifth Michigan, he was able to reclaim most of the wagons and horses recently lost, and took many Michigan men prisoner. Some of the Fifth and most of Vinton's Battalion managed to get back to Brigade lines. The rest were scattered and left to make their way to safety on their own. Captured Confederate wagons and equipment retained by the federals were brought to Custer and placed with the brigade's baggage train. Company B had been detailed as the guard and escort for the trains that day, all under the command of Captain Daniel Powers.[21]

As the Confederates pressed the Michigan Brigade, Powers sought a better place for the trains. He went to Custer and asked permission to move the trains. Lieutenant Harmon Smith of Company F, Seventh Michigan Cavalry was near Custer that day when an officer approached him and asked permission to "move certain things for safety to the rear." Custer replied, "Yes, by all means." A few moments later he stopped what he was doing, looked around and asked, "Where in hell is the rear?" By this time the officer was gone. Smith didn't know him, but it was Captain Powers. With Hampton pressing from the North, Rosser from the West, and Fitz Lee from the East, the path of least resistance was most likely to the South.[22]

As Powers and Company B left the brigade perimeter with the trains, a portion of Lee's Division charged, and after a short fight, captured the wagons, caissons, and many of the escort. At the same time, one of the guns from their artillery battery was taken. Custer gathered up Smith and his company from the Seventh, plus a few others, and recaptured the gun and a few wagons, but the rest were lost to the enemy, including Custer's headquarters wagon. His cook, a former slave named Eliza Brown, was taken as well, but she escaped that night and made it back to the Brigade.[23]

Sixth Michigan troopers fought on the western and southern sides of the perimeter, opposing Rosser's Brigade and other elements of Hampton's Division. Desperately, they continued to fight without any cover or concealment. There was a small benefit to the situation, as the rebels could not bring massed fire on the federals without hitting their own soldiers as well. Small group or individual fights occurred all over the field.[24]

Late in the afternoon, Sheridan's troops finally broke through to the Michigan Brigade, pushed the enemy away, and ended the fighting for the day. The entire federal force camped near the station that night.[25]

Next day, the Second Cavalry Division was employed tearing up track to the west. In mid-afternoon, the First Division was ordered to ride towards Gordonsville. Leading the division was the Michigan Brigade, with the Sixth in front. Just over a mile from their starting point, the enemy was engaged, and a second day of heavy fighting began. Wolverines were again facing Hampton's troopers, who were in well prepared defensive positions. All attempts to break the enemy line were repulsed, and more losses were suffered by the Michigan regiments. As the last light faded from the sky, Sheridan withdrew his force to the station. Those who were too badly wounded to be moved were left there, to the clemency of the Confederates. Having gathered all the wheeled vehicles they could commandeer in the area, the wounded that could be moved, as well as equipment and supplies, were loaded up. In the darkness, a long, painful retreat began, back to the Army of the Potomac.[26]

Moving at a moderate pace, Sheridan led his men all the way to Spotsylvania before turning southeast along the Mattapony River. As the column moved along the roads, through the heat and dust, many escaped slaves joined the march. All the vehicles that could be commandeered along the route were pressed into service. Horses gave out and had to be shot, leaving the route littered with stinking carcasses. Food for men and refugees, and forage for the animals had to be procured from farms and towns along the way, which caused hardship for the residents. All the time, Hampton was lurking nearby, looking for an opportunity to pounce on Sheridan and his overburdened column. On June 18, the slogging procession finally reached King and Queen Court House, where the wounded, prisoners, and non-combatants were taken away.

While there, it was learned the Third Cavalry Division needed help, so the long march continued across the James River to Ream's Station south of Petersburg. Upon arrival, they found the Third Division had withdrawn from danger. On July 2, the command managed to plod its way back to Lighthouse Point on the James River, where they were finally allowed to rest. It had been a grueling and costly campaign.[27]

Sixth Michigan suffered about one-hundred casualties during the two day battle at Trevilian Station. Fourteen of them were from Company B. Most, if not all of them, occurred on June 11, in defense of the baggage train. Of the fourteen, six were original members. Captured with Captain Daniel Powers were Privates Augustus Arsnoe, Homer Goucher, and Harvey Seeley. Goucher and Seeley would die in Andersonville Prison later in the year. Arsnoe survived and rejoined the company at the end of the war. Arsnoe's older brother James was wounded, for which he would receive a disability discharge the following spring. Sergeant Perley Johnson, acting as the Regimental Commissary Sergeant, was severely wounded, and would not return until December.[28]

First Sergeant Egbert Conklin was wounded in the left thigh. Sent to a hospital in Philadelphia, he would resume his duties in late November. Sergeant Stephen Stowe, also wounded in the left thigh, was captured. Taken to Crompton Hospital in Lynchburg, Stowe was joined by Private Harvey Smith, who had been badly wounded on June 11, and one of those left behind. Stowe's wound became gangrenous, and he died on July 30. Smith would recover and be released the following February. Private William Onweller died while recovering from his wound in a federal hospital on July 29. Privates

Robert Jones, Andrew McLarren, William Reynolds, and Jacob Smith were also wounded. All but Smith would return to the company.[29]

Captain Powers was taken to Charleston by a circuitous route, passing through Virginia, Georgia, and the Carolinas on the way. Arriving in late July, Powers met other captured officers from Michigan. In August he was among a large group transferred from the jail yard to a marine hospital. Two months later he was sent to a prison camp in Columbia, South Carolina. On November 24, a small group of officers, including Powers, boldly "ran the guard" and escaped. Traveling at night and hiding in woods during the day, they headed West, hoping to reach Sherman's forces around Atlanta.

Six days after escaping, the group was recaptured near Edgefield, South Carolina. When he was returned to the prison camp at Columbia on December 11, Powers learned he had been dismissed from the service on July 5 for "treachery and cowardice." When the brigade's baggage train was captured, and Custer lost his headquarters wagon for a second time, prized personal possessions including his commission as a General and rather intimate letters from his wife Libby fell into rebel hands. An embarrassed Custer blamed Powers, and asked President Lincoln for his dismissal. Powers was no longer officially in the service, but he was still a prisoner-of-war, and would not be released. The day after he heard the news, he was placed in a lunatic asylum, probably as punishment for his escape. Finally released in early March 1865, he made his own way home, battered but not broken.[30]

The Michigan Brigade spent the month of July resting and getting resupplied. It was a comfortable time for those who remained. Company B, now commanded by First Lieutenant Nelson Thomas, had about fifty men after some of the wounded returned. More promotions were made to fill vacated positions.

Effective July 1, John Fuller and Frederick Kettle became Corporals. Frank Gross was also promoted, even though he was in a hospital recovering from the wound he received in the Wilderness. Major James Kidd became Colonel James Kidd on July 9.[31]

Late in July the Michigan Brigade was part of a movement to the north of the James River, intended to take General Robert E. Lee's attention away from the area where the federals exploded a mine to break the enemy line at Petersburg. The plan failed miserably, and the siege dragged on.[32]

During June and July, Confederate forces under command of Lieutenant General Jubal Early, had marched down the Shenandoah Valley and threatened Washington. Early's Corps was still in Maryland. General Grant asked President Lincoln for permission to send a commander he trusted to the valley, to clear it of rebel troops and end its support of the Confederacy. On August 1, General Sheridan was sent to take command of an army forming for that purpose. Two days later, the Michigan Cavalry Brigade followed.[33]

NOTES

1 Kidd, 264-265

2 ibid, 265-269; Robertson, 595.

3 Kidd, 269; OR, Series I, Vol. 36, Pt. 1, 816 (Custer's report).

4 Kidd, 270-271; RSMV-36, 63.

5 Kidd, 278-279, 284-286; OR, 816-817 (Custer).

6 Kidd, 286-291.

7   ibid, 293; OR, 817 (Custer).

8   Kidd, 295-300.

9   ibid, 301-302; OR, 817-818 (Custer).

10 Kidd, 302-303.

11 ibid, 303-306; Robertson, 596-597; OR, 818-819 (Custer).

12 Kidd, 307-313; Robertson, 597; OR, 819 (Custer); RSMV-36, 100, 136.

13 Kidd, 313-315; Roberston, 597-598.

14 Kidd 313-315; OR, 820-821 (Custer).

15 Kidd, 324-327; OR, 821 (Custer); RSMV-36, 51.

16 Kidd, 329-336; OR, 822-823 (Custer).

17 Kidd, 342-343, 345; OR, 823 (Custer).

18 Kidd, 345, 348.

19 OR, 823 (Custer), 1095 (Hampton); B&L, Vol. 4, 233-234 (Rodenbough's account).

20 Kidd, 350-359.

21 ibid, 359-360; OR, 823-824 (Custer), 1095 (Hampton).

22 Lee, History of Seventh Michigan Cavalry, 230.

23 OR, 823-824 (Custer); Marguerite Merington, ed., *The Custer Story: The Life and Intimate Letters of General George A. Custer and His Wife Elizabeth*, (Lincoln: University of Nebraska Press, 1950) 104; Walbrook D. Swank, *Battle of Trevilian Station* (Shippensburg, Pa., Burd Street Press, 1994) 103 (Reminiscences of John Gill, courier on staff of Fitzhugh Lee).

24 OR, 823-824.

25 ibid; Kidd, 360-361; B&L, Vol. 4, 234.

26   Kidd, 361-364; OR, 824 (Custer), 1096-1097 (Hampton).

27   Kidd, 369-370; OR, 825 (Custer); Swank, 107-109 (Recollections of Samuel B. Rucker, 6th Va. Cav., POW).

28   Kidd 364-365; RSMV-36, 16, 36, 61, 77, 78, 90, 103, 111, 115, 122, 127, 135; Diary entry for Daniel Powers, June 11, 1864.

29   Military Service Record for Egbert S. Conklin (Medical Records and notations on Muster Rolls), Records of the Adjutant General's Office, Record Group 94, National Archives, Washington, D.C.; Declaration for Widow's Pension, Jane Stowe Osterhout, Widow of Stephen L. Stowe, Civil War Pension Application File WC 65179, SC 113909 (Statement by Harvey Smith), Records of the Veterans Administration, Record Group 15, National Archives, Washington, D.C. After the war, Stowe's body was reburied in Poplar Grove National Cemetery, Grave 4965, Petersburg National Battlefield; RSMV-36, 36, 78, 90, 103, 115, 127, 135.

30   Merington, 103-105; Swank, 72-73 (Edward L. Wells account, 4th S.C. Cav.); Diary entries and correspondence for Daniel Powers, June 12– December 12, 1864; Military Service Record for Daniel H. Powers, Records of the Adjutant General's Office, Record Group 94, National Archives, Washington, D.C.

31   Kidd, 370, 372; RSMV-36. 57, 63, 81.

32   Kidd, 371.

33   ibid, 373.

THE SHENANDOAH
VALLEY

Loaded on transports and shipped along Chesapeake
Bay to the Potomac River, the Michigan Cavalry Brigade
landed in Washington, D.C. on August 6. Before the campaign even began, Company B suffered its first campaign loss.
Sergeant Edwin Whitney had been sick in the Cavalry Corps
hospital. When he recovered, he was sent to the dismounted
camp at the capital. Whitney was detailed as part of the guard
for Edward's Ferry, up the Potomac River from Washington.
On July 26, Confederate raiders swooped down upon the ferry,
capturing some of the guards, including Whitney. Prisoners
from the raid were taken to Mount Jackson in the Shenandoah
Valley. Twelve days later, as the Sixth Michigan was landing
in Washington, Whitney escaped and traveled in a northwesterly direction, across the mountains and over rough terrain
to the nearest friendly forces. He reached safety in Ohio on
September 5, and reported to a district Provost Marshal there.
Within a week, he was recovered and on his way back to his
unit.[1]

Sergeant Elliott Norton was promoted away from Company
B during this period. Earlier in the year he had been the acting
Regimental Sergeant-Major. His abilities were noted, and on
August 7, he was mustered into service as a Second Lieutenant
in Company H. Later, in January 1865, he would be appointed

a First Lieutenant and made Regimental Adjutant. Another loss was Private Charles Post, who died of disease in Washington on August 27, and was buried in Arlington Cemetery.[2]

Marching through Maryland, the Michigan Brigade crossed the Potomac at Harper's Ferry on the way to Halltown, where they arrived on August 10. From there, they began their first operation as part of General Sheridan's Army of the Shenandoah. First Division Commander, Major General Alfred Torbert, was elevated to command of all cavalry for the valley army. Brigadier General Wesley Merritt was promoted to command of the First Division.[3]

For the next two weeks, Michigan troopers marched and scouted the valley between Winchester, Strasburg, Front Royal, and back to Berryville, occasionally skirmishing with the rebels. On August 16, a battalion of the Sixth Michigan commanded by Captain Harvey Vinton, deployed on foot as skirmishers, fought Confederate infantry and cavalry near Front Royal. Vinton's men repulsed an enemy assault and counter-attacked, taking many prisoners.[4]

After Confederate forces in the valley were reinforced, Sheridan began to withdraw his army toward the Potomac River. Near Leetown, federal cavalry unexpectedly encountered rebel infantry on August 25. After a brisk fight, Torbert fell back to the east, leaving the Michigan Brigade as a rear guard. Just as they were about to withdraw themselves, the Wolverines discovered they were cut off and nearly surrounded. Enemy infantry forced them back into a perimeter near Sheperdstown, with their backs against the Potomac. Under Custer's direction, the brigade fought a brilliant retrograde action, while a little known ford was found. Fifth and Sixth Michigan held the rebels back as the rest crossed to Maryland. Kidd's regiment was then ordered to cross, followed by the Fifth. After reaching safety, many Michigan cavalrymen held the opinion that

General Torbert made no effort to learn of their predicament or support them, and therefore had abandoned them to the enemy.[5]

Three days later, the Brigade rejoined the Division at Leetown, after Early's Confederate Army had withdrawn from the northern end of the valley. Next day, the Sixth was involved in a fight at Smithfield, where Private Oscar Stout was wounded in the right arm and side. Company B suffered another loss the following day, August 30, when Private William Tuffs, one of the company's teamsters, was taken prisoner near Berryville.[6]

Cavalry activities for the first half of September included marching up and down the valley, doing picket duty, scouting, escorting wagon trains, and laying in camp.[7]

Early on the morning of September 19, as part of a major operation, the Sixth was tasked to secure a crossing over Opequan Creek at Lock's Ford. The regiment dismounted and advanced in columns to the creek. After crossing, the men deployed into line under fire, and charged across an open field toward a fortified enemy position. Reaching some farm buildings, the Sixth began to concentrate fire on the rebels as the First and Seventh prepared to make a mounted charge. Just as all units were ready to attack, another federal brigade appeared on the enemy's flank, forcing them to withdraw.[8]

After reforming, the Michigan Brigade helped push the Confederates down the Martinsburg Pike toward Winchester. Michigan troopers were again facing old foes of Fitzhugh Lee's Division, who by mid-afternoon had set up a defensive line north of town. All of First Cavalry Division charged, breaking the enemy cavalry and driving them from the field. Suddenly confronted by rebel infantry, the cavalry charged again, but was thrown back. Reforming and charging a third time, they broke the Confederate line, and during the initial pursuit the Sixth went on to capture more prisoners than it had men engaged in the fight. One of the Sixth's casualties was Colonel Kidd, who had been slightly wounded in the leg. Company B suffered no losses.[9]

For the next week, federal horsemen, including those from Michigan, chased the Confederates up the valley. Private James Neal was wounded in a skirmish at Fisher's Hill on September 21. Three days later there was a sharp fight with enemy cavalry, who were quickly driven away. On September 26, Brigadier General George A. Custer relinquished command of the Michigan Cavalry Brigade after being given leadership of a cavalry division. In consequence, Colonel Kidd took temporary command of the brigade, leaving the Sixth under the direction of Major Charles Deane. That same day, Deane led the regiment in an attempt to capture a rebel supply train near Port Republic. During the approach, they found Early's entire army defending it. Kidd reported that the Sixth "judiciously failed to capture the train."[10]

Remaining in the vicinity of Port Republic for about ten days, the regiment added cattle herding and mill operations to their list of activities. Colonel Kidd decided to use the grist mills to supply some of his brigade's needs. This was discovered by General Merritt, who angrily ordered the work to cease and the mills burned. Kidd, and his men, learned about total war through this incident. Kidd later wrote, "It was disagreeable business and – we can be frank now – I did not relish it." This was the beginning of a retrograde movement by the federal army. As it moved back down the valley, livestock were taken or destroyed, and all crops and structures of use to the rebels were burned.[11]

As the cavalrymen marched through, destroying valley resources, they were followed by outraged Confederate horsemen commanded by another old adversary, Brigadier General Thomas Rosser, who sniped at and harassed the federals at every opportunity. On October 9, the Yankees turned to fight at Tom's Brook. After battling hard for about two hours, the

rebel lines were broken and a running fight ensued, covering many miles. In a reversal of the Buckland episode of a
year before, the battle was nicknamed the "Woodstock Races."
Ending their trail of devastation, the Army of the Shenandoah
went into camp along Cedar Creek the following day. General
Early and his Confederate army followed within a few days,
looking for an opportunity to strike back.[12]

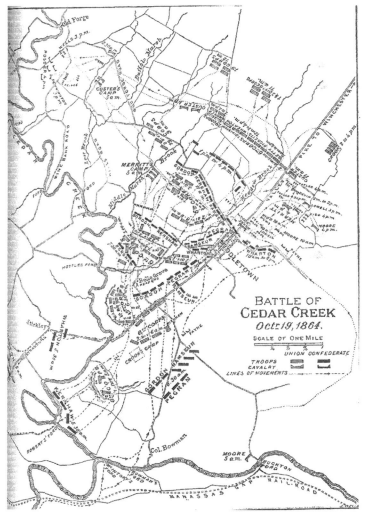

From Battles and Leaders of th Civil War,
ed. Robert Underwood and Clarence Buel

Before a week had passed, Sheridan and the Cavalry Corps were riding back to Front Royal. From there, Sheridan went to a conference in Washington, and the cavalry was to raid in the area of Charlottesville. Just before the raid was to begin, Sheridan called it off and sent the troopers back to Cedar Creek.

On the morning of October 19, Early's Army attacked, over-running the infantry camps and pushing the federals back about two miles. The Michigan Cavalry Brigade was on the far right at the beginning of the attack, and wasn't actively engaged. As the battle progressed, the Brigade began moving to the left, and by mid-morning was in position with the rest of the First Cavalry Division just behind the left of the main lines. In the early afternoon, Sheridan arrived on the field, after his storied ride, and began directing operations. Preparations were made for an assault to regain the pillaged camps and reverse the tide of battle.[13]

Under fire much of the time, the Michigan horsemen waited in mounted formation for the order to attack. At about four in the afternoon, it was given. Men had to advance over broken terrain, which made the task more difficult. The first assault was repulsed. A second attempt reached a point just short of the main rebel line when the infantry was thrown back, forcing the cavalry to retire with them. Charging for a third time, federal troops finally broke the Confederate line, causing Early to retreat with only remnants of his army. Chasing rebels as far as the North Branch of the Shenandoah River, a distance of about three miles, the Sixth Michigan took many prisoners. Private John Burder was killed in action that afternoon – Company B's price of victory.[14]

What was left of the Confederate Army in the valley retreated all the way to New Market. Pursuit began the following day. First Cavalry Division rode as far as Woodstock and halted. Patrols were sent out, and skirmish lines set up, but there was no sign of an aggressive move by the Confederates. After a few days, the cavalry returned to their camps at Cedar Creek. In November, the brigade moved to Winchester and set up winter quarters.

During the winter months, the Michigan Brigade participated in operations in the Shenandoah and Loudon Valleys searching for rebel guerillas and destroying any property of use to the enemy. Confederate Major John Mosby and his command seemed to conduct a private war against the Michigan cavalrymen, and attacked stragglers, pickets, and guards whenever possible. Private Isaac (Ike) Church of Company B was taken prisoner in December. Despite the dangers on routine duties, camp life was pleasant enough. General Custer and other officers had their wives visit them in camp. At that time, Custer took steps to have another family member join him.[15]

After he had taken command of the Third Cavalry Division, Custer wrote a letter to Major General George Thomas, the "Rock of Chickamauga," requesting his brother, Thomas Custer of the Twenty-First Ohio Infantry, be transferred to Sheridan's command so he could accept a commission in Company B of the Sixth Michigan Cavalry. A vacancy existed due to the disability discharge of Second Lieutenant Charles Parker in September. Tom Custer was mustered in as a Second Lieutenant on November 8, retroactive to July 11. Quartermaster Sergeant James Johnson was also commissioned a Second Lieutenant on January 10, 1865. On February 3, First Lieutenant Nelson Thomas was promoted to Captain, and Second Lieutenant Alexander Cook of Company C, who had been wounded at Shepherdstown, was promoted to First Lieutenant and assigned to Company B. Johnson's and

GEORGE, TOM, & ELIZABETH CUSTER

Photo Courtesy of the State Archives of Michigan

Cook's promotions were effective back to December 10. On paper, the company's officer contingent was full. The reality was somewhat different.[16]

Lieutenant Tom Custer spent little, if any, time with Company B. He was immediately detailed to his brother's staff, where he remained to the end of the war. Cook's wound continued to plague him, and it is not clear how long he was actually with the company in the field. He was discharged for disability on May 15, leaving Captain Thomas and Lieutenant Johnson as the only officers serving with the unit.[17]

Some enlisted men in the company were also promoted during the valley campaign. On September 1, Privates Asa Baker and Philip Cunningham were made Corporals. Baker was the first of the 1864 recruits to be promoted. Corporal John Newton was raised to Sergeant on October 1, as was "Wash" Stewart on the first day of November. February 1, 1865 was a big promotion day for Company B. Richard Moore and Joshua Beaman, two more of the 1864 recruits, made Corporal. Ezra Brown and David Caywood were elevated to Sergeant. Caywood took over as Company Commissary Sergeant, replacing Perley Johnson who was now the Regimental Commissary Sergeant. That same day, David McVean became the Quartermaster Sergeant, filling the vacancy left when James Johnson was promoted.[18]

Company B lost men to disease and disability as well as combat, and there was a need for more recruits, but a recruiting drive was not conducted until March 1865. Two men enlisted into the company in August, Nathan Aldrich and Joseph English, but English transferred to Company M in February. In that February, Charles Bloomburg and Ezra Mead were enlisted at Jackson, Michigan, and William McGee and Frank Eaton signed up in Kalamazoo County, but none of them would join the unit until after it had left the valley. Some of the wounded returned while the Sixth was at Winchester. One had to be escorted back.

After being wounded in late August, Private Oscar Stout was sent to hospitals in Baltimore and Philadelphia. In October, Oscar was sent home for a twenty day furlough. When time expired, he had not reported in. Declared a deserter for a second time, Oscar was arrested by military authorities at his home in Cedar Springs and taken to Detroit. He was put aboard a train which arrived in Washington on Christmas Day, 1864.

Oscar was returned to the company for duty in late January 1865 – ever the reluctant warrior.[19]

On a cold and rainy February 27, the Michigan Brigade left its winter camps for the last time. General Torbert had been replaced by General Merritt, and Brigadier General Thomas Devin was promoted to command of the First Cavalry Division. The Sixth Michigan Cavalry marched under the leadership of Lieutenant Colonel Harvey Vinton. Colonel Kidd had been serving on a court-martial board during the winter, and could not get Sheridan to relieve him of that duty so he could be with his regiment. There was friction between Kidd and Colonel Peter Stagg of the First Michigan because they had competed for command of the brigade. Kidd was senior in rank, but Stagg had served with the army longer, and convinced General Merritt that he should be in command. Kidd would rejoin the Sixth later.[20]

Three federal divisions marched south over muddy roads to Woodstock, and then on to Staunton. Brushing aside the remnants of Rosser's cavalry, Sheridan's force drove on to Waynesboro, where what was left of Early's army was easily destroyed on March 2. Sheridan had accomplished his mission. The Shenandoah Valley was cleared of any effective Confederate force. Mosby's Battalion was merely an annoyance. Leaving the valley for good, Sheridan and his troops marched through Rockfish Gap the next day.[21]

NOTES

1   OR, Series 1, Vol. 43, Pt. 1, 463,(Kidd's report); Military Service Record for Edwin E. Whitney (Notes on descriptive list, Sept 1864), Records of the Adjutant General's Office, Record Group 94, National Archives, Washington D.C.

2   RSMV-36, 102, 110; Military Service Record for Elliott M. Norton (Notes on muster rolls), Records of the Adjutant General's Office, Record Group 94, National Archives, Washington, D.C.

3   OR, 463-466 (Kidd's and Deane's reports); Kidd, 378.

4   OR, 464 (Kidd), 466 (Deane); Kidd, 374-377.

5   OR, 464 (Kidd), 466 (Deane): Kidd, 378-383.

6   OR, 466 (Dean); Military Service Records for Oscar Stout and William J. Tuffs (Notes on muster rolls), Records of the Adjutant General's Office, Record Group 94, National Archives, Washington, D.C.

7   OR, 466-467 (Deane).

8   OR, 454-455 (Custer), 464 (Kidd), 467 (Deane); Kidd, 385-389.

9   OR, 455-459 (Custer), 465 (Kidd), 467 (Deane); Kidd 389-393.

10   RSMV-36, 99; OR, 465 (Kidd), 467 (Deane); Kidd 396-397.

11   OR, 467 (Deane); Kidd, 397-399.

12   OR, 465 (Kidd); Kidd 399-402.

13   Kidd, 407-421.

14   OR, 465 (Kidd); Kidd 421-424; RSMV-36, 29.

15   OR, 671-672 (Merritt); RSMV-36, 33.

16   RSMV-36, 37, 42, 77, 138.

17   Order Book, Regimental Special Order #37, November 20, 1864, and Cavalry Corps Special Order #12, November 14, 1864; RSMV-36, 37.

18   RSMV-36, 18, 21, 27, 31, 42, 90, 100, 133.

19   ibid, 14, 23, 50, 51, 89, 93; Military Service Record for Oscar Stout, (Documents and notations on muster rolls).

20   RSMV-36, 45, 143; OR, Series I, Vol. 46, Pt. 1, 488 (Devin), 495 (Stagg).

21   B&L, Vol. 4, 521 (Merritt's account); OR 488-489 (Devin), 495 (Stagg).

APPOMATTOX AND THE GRAND REVIEW

On March 4, the day after riding across the Blue Ridge, Sheridan's cavalry column arrived in Charlottesville. Together with other units in Merritt's command, the Michigan Brigade was again engaged in the necessary evil of taking or destroying any property of use to the Confederates. After tearing up railroad tracks running toward Lynchburg, the federal horsemen cut a swath southeast to Columbia, Virginia, on the James River. Rain and cool temperatures added physical discomfort to the unpleasant tasks. Moving in an easterly direction from Columbia, Sheridan's two cavalry divisions destroyed canal locks and boats, mills, dams, bridges, produce, and anything that could be used to support the rebel war effort. Passing to the north of Richmond, the column turned southeast once again at Hanover Court House, riding along the Pamunkey River to White House, where the "raid" ended on March 19. Very little resistance was encountered, as the Confederates could not spare many troops from the defenses of Richmond and Petersburg.[1]

Sheridan officially reported to General Grant at City Point on March 23. With the additional troops, Grant developed plans to force the enemy out of his entrenchments and bring the war to an end.

On March 29, the Cavalry Corps marched around the southern end of Confederate defenses protecting Petersburg. At the end of a difficult trek over muddy roads, federal horsemen camped at Dinwiddie Court House. A reconnaissance of Five Forks was made next day by a force which included

Virginia Campaigns

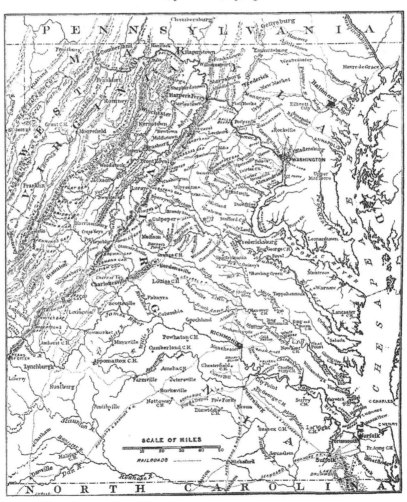

From Battles and Leaders of the Civil War, Ed. Robert
Underwood and Clarence Buel

the Michigan Brigade. Five Forks was a major road junction that enabled Confederate forces besieged in Richmond and Petersburg to protect the Southside Railway, which was one of their last open supply routes. Rain hampered the operation, but rebel infantry, supported by cavalry and artillery, was discovered in defensive positions.[2]

When dawn arrived on March 31, the rain came to an end. Sheridan began to move his cavalry on the enemy defenses. Infantry support for the cavalry, for many reasons, was slow to arrive. Instead of waiting for the federal assault, a Confederate infantry division commanded by Major General George Pickett, of Gettysburg fame, and cavalry led by Fitzhugh Lee, made a spoiling attack on the federals. The Michigan Cavalry Brigade, along with other units, was forced steadily back by the heavy onslaught. Fighting dismounted over a distance of about two miles, the Wolverines were able to maintain their unit integrity. Finally breaking away from the enemy, who followed in close pursuit, they were compelled to ride a wide loop back to Dinwiddie. There they joined the rest of Sheridan's command defending a half-moon perimeter above the village. As daylight faded, the rebels broke off the fight.[3]

By morning on April 1, federal infantry still had not arrived, but Pickett's troops were gone – back to their defensive works in front of Five Forks. Against light resistance, Sheridan again advanced his troopers. First Cavalry Division, with the Michigan Brigade leading, crossed Chamberlain's Creek and moved to a position from which they could launch an assault. Sheridan waited most of the day for the infantry to come up and get into position. Finally, late in the afternoon, bugles sounded the charge as dismounted cavalrymen moved on the right and center of the enemy line, while the infantry attacked the rebel left. Against stubborn resistance, foot soldiers of Fifth Corps smashed the enemy flank, and the entire line crumbled.

Infantrymen and cavalrymen were thrown together in a final thrust, which destroyed the Confederate force. Hundreds of prisoners were taken.[4]

Merritt's command, including the Michigan Brigade, moved on the Southside Railroad next day against light, sporadic resistance, and destroyed as much track as they could. That same day, April 2, General Grant launched a general assault on the Confederate lines. General Robert E. Lee was forced to abandon the defenses of Richmond and Petersburg and made a desperate dash to the west.[5]

April 3 was spent marching in pursuit. Troopers of the Michigan Brigade spent most of the next day skirmishing with remnants of Pickett's and Bushrod Johnson's Confederate infantry divisions. Well after dark, the men mounted up and made a night march, arriving at Jetersville around noon. Later in the day, they were relieved by infantry troops and camped in the rear of the army for a much needed rest.

On the following morning, April 6, while on the march near Rice's Station, a rebel supply train was encountered, protected by infantry. While most of Merritt's command engaged Pickett's and Johnson's divisions again, the Michigan Cavalry Brigade was deployed on the far right in support of Sixth Corps along Sailor's Creek. Charging in on the flank of enemy infantry, the Wolverines took about three hundred prisoners and routed the rest. Pursuit continued past dark, until stiff resistance was met on the upper reaches of the creek. First Cavalry Division then fell back about a mile and made camp around midnight.[6]

On the morning of April 7, the horse soldiers were on the road again, marching beyond Prince Edward Court House before stopping for the night. Next day the march resumed to Appomattox Station, where Custer's Third Cavalry Division was engaged in a sharp fight. Dismounting, the Michigan

Brigade advanced in support and helped drive the rebels back on Appomattox Court House. As April 9 dawned, the still dismounted Wolverines lined up to launch an attack. Confederate infantry, supported by Fitz Lee's command, moved out from Appomattox Court House and drove the cavalrymen back. At that moment, hard marching federal infantry arrived on the scene, forcing the enemy troops to withdraw, and signaling an end to any rebel hopes of fighting through to the west. Devin's troopers remounted and moved to the right flank, in preparation for another attack, just as a cease fire was declared about noon. Surrender of the Confederate Army of Northern Virginia took place later that day. Camp was made and night was spent in position on the final battlefield.[7]

Federal soldiers mingled with former Confederates that evening. Food was shared, and men on both sides engaged in a subdued celebration of the end of hostilities, and their own survival. Within days, most of the ex-rebels were home or on their way there.[8]

On the day following the surrender, First Cavalry Division was sent to Prospect Station, southeast of Appomattox Court House. During that eventful spring, the cavalry was kept busy making sure there were no more pockets of organized resistance. Danville, Virginia was suspected of being a rebel rendezvous point, so the Michigan Brigade was sent there late in April. After President Lincoln's assassination, the U.S. government was very sensitive to rumors of armed groups of southerners. During April and May of 1865, most Confederate troops were surrendered and disbanded. General Meade's Army of the Potomac, including the Michigan Cavalry Brigade, then marched to Washington, D.C. to participate in their Grand review on May 23. Major General William T. Sherman's Army of the Tennessee and Army of the Ohio paraded on May 24.[9]

The Sixth Michigan Cavalry suffered very little loss during its final campaign of the Civil War. Company B did not lose a man to combat or sickness. Instead, the unit gained thirteen enlistees in March. Those men are listed below with their home towns or places of enlistment:

Daniel Dooley – Jackson
Peter Durham – Assyria, Barry County
Alson Evans – Jackson
Samuel E. Fisher – Battle Creek
Lewis L. Flint – Battle Creek
Schofield Furnier – Benton, Washtenaw County
Joseph M. Sanders – Jackson
Joseph Smith – Pontiac
John C. Thomson – Battle Creek
Anthony Trumbley – Benton, Washtenaw County
Edward N. Walker – Grand Rapids
Morris E.N. Wright – Battle Creek
Myndert Yeomans – Maple Grove, Barry County

These men joined the unit when it was in Washington preparing for the Grand Review. They endured rough treatment, or were completely ignored, except for the purpose of duty. The old-timers, and recruits of 1864, had been through too much to appreciate "late comers." All the dirty details went to the new men. Two original members were promoted after the Danville expedition. On May 1, James Cronkright made Corporal, and Solon Bentley became a Sergeant. There were plenty of non-commissioned officers in the company to supervise the recruits.[10]

One member of Company B covered himself in glory during the last days of the war. Second Lieutenant Thomas W. Custer won two Medals of Honor in early April of 1865. He managed to capture two enemy battle flags on April 2 and April 6, while detailed as a member of his brother's staff. Wounded slightly during one episode, he remained on duty.[11]

Troopers of Company B, as well as the rest of the Sixth Michigan Cavalry, were looking forward to going home. Their job was done and the unpleasantness finished – or so they thought. On May 21, before the Grand Review, Lieutenant General U.S. Grant ordered First Brigade, First Cavalry Division to report to Major General John Pope at St. Louis. Most of the men were not aware of the orders, or there might have been a mutiny. On May 24 and 25, the men boarded trains bound for Parkersburg, West Virginia. Many of them thought it was the first leg of the long trip home. The Governor of Michigan, Henry Crapo, had said as much when he spoke to them just before they left Washington. But it was not to be. There was to be one more campaign.[12]

NOTES

1   OR, Series I, Vol. 46, Pt. 1, 495-496 (Stagg's report).

2   OR, 1122 (Devin).

3   OR, 1122-1123 (Devin), 1299 (Fitzhugh Lee); B&L, Vol. 4, 710-711 (Porter's account).

4   OR, 1123-1124 (Devin), 1299-1300 (F. Lee); B&L, Vol. 4, 711-714 (Porter).

5   OR, 1124-1125 (Devin), 1300 (F. Lee); B&L, Vol. 4, 716-718 (Porter).

6   OR, 1125-1126 (Devin), 1302-1303 (F. Lee); B&L, Vol. 4, 721-722 (Keifer's account).

7   OR, 1126 (Devin), 1303 (F. Lee).

8   B&L, Vol. 4, 745 (Porter).

9   OR, 1126 (Devin); B&L, Vol. 4, 755-758 (Slocum's account), 768 (Editor's notes).

10   RSMV-36, 22, 41, 47, 49, 52, 54, 55, 58, 120, 128, 138, 140, 144, 154; *Grand Rapids Daily Eagle,* June 19, 1865, 2 (Letter from Chaplain Greeley).

11   RSMV-36, 42-43; OR, 1258 (List of Medal of Honor winners).

12   OR, Vol. 48, Pt. 2, 526 (Grant's order); *Grand Rapids Daily Eagle,* June 3, 1865, 1 (by A.N.B.), June 19, 1865, 2 (Greeley's Letter).

ON THE GREAT PLAINS

Arriving at Parkersburg after a three day train ride, men of the Michigan Cavalry Brigade, and some of their mounts, were crammed onto river steamers and paddled down the Ohio River. A few men held hope they were on their way home. Most of them began to believe rumors of a western campaign against rebel hold-outs or Indians. All wanted to be discharged. Optimistic Chaplain Stephen Greeley was probably the only man in the regiment who enjoyed the boat ride.[1]

Late in the day on June 1, the boats pulled into the docks at St. Louis. Recently promoted Brigadier General Peter Stagg reported next day to Major General John Pope, commander of the vast Military Division of the Missouri. Pope immediately ordered Stagg and his brigade to Fort Leavenworth in Kansas, which was the headquarters of Major General Grenville Dodge, commander of the Department of the Missouri – part of Pope's realm. While at St. Louis, men who had been wounded or captured during the war, and were fit for duty, rejoined the brigade. Colonel Kidd was relieved of his duty on the court-martial board and rode a train to St. Louis where he took command of the Sixth again.[2]

Departing on the morning of June 3, the Sixth Michigan and part of the Fifth were transported up the Missouri River on one boat – the Lizzie Gill. Crowded conditions were made worse by hot weather. Some men became ill and were left along the way, with orders to proceed to Leavenworth when they recovered. Three days after leaving St. Louis, thankful yet still disgruntled horse soldiers debarked from the river steamer and set up camp on the prairie beyond the fort. Dust and wind made camp conditions more than unpleasant.[3]

Having only 600 mounts for 2300 troopers in the brigade, General Pope supplied them with 1600 more horses, which was additional evidence of continued service. Senior officers feared mass desertions or mutiny. Colonel Kidd, with the help of the other officers, worked hard to keep the regiment calm and together.[4]

General Dodge finally gave orders for the brigade to proceed along the Military Road and Oregon Trail to Julesburg, in Colorado Territory, where they would receive further instructions. Leading the way, the Sixth began their march on June 17. Seven days later the First and Seventh Michigan Regiments followed, under command of General Stagg. A contingent of the Sixth, lead by Captain Benjamin Rockafellow of Company I accompanied Stagg's column. Lieutenant Johnson of Company B was with Rockafellow's group.[5]

Original members of Company A of the Sixth, who had been initially recruited for the Fifth Michigan and had been in service longer, were discharged with the Fifth on June 21. This group included Chaplain Greeley of the Sixth. Some members of the First Michigan had served even longer, but had reenlisted in 1864, and were obliged to remain. Small detachments from the First, Sixth, and Seventh Regiments stayed at Fort Leavenworth. These detachments were made up of men who were detailed to key jobs or were not physically able to make the long march west. Soldiers from Company B who remained at Leavenworth and discharged earlier than the others included Privates Abel Blood, George Labell, Jacob

Vanetten, Solon Baxter, Calvin Glazier, John Green, Daniel Fuller, Daniel Stewart, and Oscar Stout. Blood, Fuller, Stewart, and Stout were discharged on July 10, and went home together. Oscar was finally free to go home to his beloved Elizabeth and stay there, without anyone coming after him.[6]

After a week of marching through typical plains weather of sun, cloudbursts, and incessant wind, the Sixth reached Marysville, Kansas and the Oregon Trail, on Friday, June 23. Citizens of Marysville welcomed the regiment and were very hospitable, yet there were problems. That night, three of the 1864 recruits, James Jones, John Milton, and John Swarthout, led by Henry Welch, an original member of the company, deserted. They took Captain Thomas' pistols, horse, and other possessions, as well as horses and equipment belonging to other officers. All four men were charged with desertion, and Welch was dishonorably discharged. Some of their comrades were pleased to have them gone. Allen Pease wrote, "For my part I am glad they are gone for they were the meanest pups in the ranch." More men would desert later.[7]

Continuing along the trail, which had become monotonous and wearisome, the Sixth reached Fort Kearny, on the Platte River in Nebraska Territory. There they celebrated the Fourth of July in a subdued and reflective way, remembering where they had been and what had occurred on or around that date in previous years. Following the southern bank of the Platte, the march continued next day. Stagg's column arrived at Kearny on July 8, three days behind Kidd and the Sixth. Captain Rockafellow got Stagg's permission for his contingent to ride on and catch up with their regiment. By adding three or more hours of marching time each day, Rockafellow's group caught up on July 12. Three days later, the Sixth camped at Julesburg.[8]

Courthouse Rock and Jail Rock near the Oregon Trail in northwestern Nebraska

While there, Kidd received orders from Stagg to proceed to Fort Laramie as fast as possible. The First and Seventh Regiments were to be placed to protect the roads along and northwest of the South Platte River. Colonel Kidd led the Sixth out of Julesburg on July 17 and cut across country to the North Platte to pick up the Oregon Trail again. On the way to Scotts Bluff and Fort Mitchell, the regimental colors were planted on Court House Rock and Chimney Rock, well known landmarks along the trail. Rattlesnakes were a constant problem, on the trail and especially in camp. Dozens of them were killed around the tents. On July 25, thirty-eight days out from Fort Leavenworth, Colonel Kidd and the Sixth Michigan Cavalry arrived at Fort Laramie and reported to Brigadier General Patrick Connor.[9]

Chimney Rock along the Oregon Trail in northwestern Nebraska

General Connor commanded the District of the Plains, part of General Dodge's Department. Connor's first impression of the Sixth was not favorable, and it did not improve with time. Many of the men had thrown away or sold their carbines in protest of their continued service. Although they kept their pistols for personal protection, without carbines they would be of little use in the expedition Connor had planned.[10]

Soldiers of the Sixth Michigan were angry, and there was no changing it. After nearly three years of hard and costly service battling and defeating Confederates, whom they considered a "worthy" foe, they felt they had earned the right to go home. They had not signed up for this. Several other cavalry units in the federal army with less time in service and fewer battle honors had been released. They could not understand why they had been chosen to trudge hundreds of miles out into the wilderness and fight Indians. Regular Army units, along with western volunteer regiments could shoulder the burden, they reasoned.[11]

**FORT LARAMIE, WYOMING
MOST OF THE BUILDINGS IN THIS ROW EXISTED
AT THE TIME OF THE POWDER RIVER CAMPAIGN**

On the other side, Plains Indians had experienced enough of soldiers, especially of the western variety. An attack on Black Kettle's peaceful village of Southern Cheyenne and Southern Arapaho by Colorado volunteer cavalry the previous November was a direct cause of the troubles along the plains' roads in 1865, along with a growing resistance by the Lakota Sioux, Northern Cheyenne, and Northern Arapaho to encroachment. A different type of guerilla war exploded across the northern Great Plains, and troopers from Michigan, unprepared and unwilling, were thrust into it.[12]

On the day after the Sixth arrived at Fort Laramie, a large war party attacked a supply train bound for Platte Bridge Station (Casper, Wyoming), and their relief force, killing many soldiers. One of the soldiers killed was Lieutenant Caspar Collins of the Eleventh Ohio Cavalry, whose name would be given, with a slight spelling variation, to the town that would grow there. Connor ordered Kidd to send five companies to relieve the units of the Eleventh Kansas Cavalry then protecting the stations guarding the trail and telegraph line between Fort Laramie and Platte Bridge. Despite not being fully armed, another four companies of the Sixth were ordered prepared to depart on the Powder River Expedition under Connor's command. Captain William

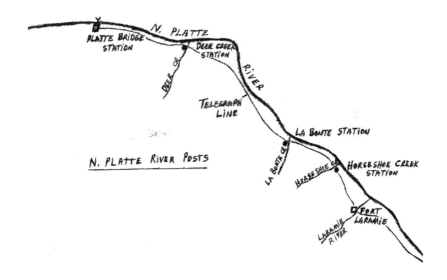

Creevey was to take his Company C, along with Companies B, D, E, and L to the stations. Companies F, H, I, and M were to go on the expedition commanded by Captain Rockafellow, with Kidd along as assistant to Connor. Companies A, G, & K were to remain at Fort Laramie.[13]

Company A, having been decimated by discharges of its original members, had men transferred from other companies to fill its ranks. Privates Daniel Dooley, Robert Jones, George McCollum, and Joseph Smith went from B to A. Company B was then down to two officers and about fifty enlisted men, including those who were sick or on detail.[14]

On July 27, Kidd left Fort Laramie to relieve the garrison at Platte Bridge Station. Nine companies marched in the evening and camped about six miles from the fort. After another day's march, the column camped near Horse Shoe Creek Station, where Company D was placed. Next day, Kidd and the remaining eight companies reached LaBonte Station, where Company C took up residence, and from where Captain Creevey would supervise all the stations. Camp was made about a mile beyond LaBonte. While there, Kidd was instructed by Connor to stay where he was and await further orders. Two days later, those orders arrived. Captain Nelson Thomas would take his Company B, along with E and L, and relieve Deer Creek and Platte Bridge Stations. Kidd would command the Left Column of the Powder River Expedition, including Rockafellow's Battalion.[15]

Company B occupied Deer Creek Station. Captain Thomas then took E and L to Platte Bridge and left them there under First Lieutenant John Molloy of Company E, and returned to Deer Creek. Escorting supply trains and making mail runs were the primary duties troopers had at the tiny, isolated posts. Stations were also manned by detachments of U.S. Volunteers, which were former Confederate prisoners who opted for federal service in the west over rotting in a prison camp. There was constant danger of Indian attacks, which restricted hunting somewhat, but did not stop it, as it was the best area for game some men had ever seen. Troopers were always careful to keep their horses well guarded. They knew the Indians valued horses as a sign of wealth and prowess against enemies.[16]

126

**PLATTE BRIDGE STATION,
CASPER, WYOMING**

While troopers at the stations settled into a routine, Rockafellow's Battalion proceeded under Kidd on Connor's expedition. Connor's column, made up Ohio, Iowa, and California troops, followed the North Platte and met with Kidd and Rockafellow near LaBonte. Together they marched northwest toward the Powder River. Kidd had made it clear to Connor that he and his regiment expected to be released from service, according to War Department directives, on or before their three years were up in October. This created additional tension for the men as they marched deeper into Indian country.

Jim Bridger and Mitch Boyer were among the civilian guides for Connor. Frank North and his hard fighting Pawnee scouts were also with the column. On August 10, Connor's force reached the Powder River. Next day, after marching along the river for about fifteen miles, they halted and set up camp on table land on the west bank near a major Indian trail and river-crossing. Three days later, on August 14, Kidd was ordered to establish Fort Connor. General Order Number One was published next day. An area twenty miles square was marked off as a military reservation, and Michigan troops began con-structing a fort.

On August 20, Pawnee Scouts were engaged in a fight with hostile Sioux and Cheyenne north of the post. Kidd was ordered to send troops out to assist Captain North. Shortly after leaving camp, thirty men from the Sixth met North and some of his scouts, whose horses were exhausted and could not continue the fight. North urged them to go after the hostiles. Riding about ten more miles, they spotted what appeared to be nearly a thousand Indians. The Michigan troops turned around and made a fast trip back to camp. This infuriated Captain North, but nobody in the Sixth was going to foolishly risk those odds when they were so close to going home.

Companies A and G arrived on August 21, escorting a supply train. Next day, Connor took his expedition north in search of hostile Indians, and left Colonel Kidd and the Sixth Michigan to build the fort - much to their relief. Confident they could handle any possible trouble, they indulged in fre-quent hunting trips.[17]

Support missions were conducted from the fort. Occasional patrols were sent out to watch the trail and surrounding area for Indian traffic. Mail runs were made to various locations, and escorts were provided for travelers through the region. James Sawyers arrived at the post leading a wagon train with min-ing equipment, tools, and machinery bound for Virginia City. General Connor ordered Colonel Kidd to provide an escort for Sawyers to the Little Big Horn River. On the afternoon of

August 26, Captain (Acting Major) Don Lovell, accompanied by Captain Osmer Cole and Lieutenant Robert Moon, departed with Sawyers' train. Two days later, Captain James Kellogg, nephew of Congressman Kellogg, rode out with a mail detail for General Connor's column, somewhere to the north.[18]

THE MARKER FOR FORT RENO (CONNOR)
BUILT BY THE SIXTH MICHIGAN CAVALRY

VIEW FROM THE MARKER LOOKING EAST
THE POWDER RIVER CAN BE SEEN IN THE DISTANCE

129

Some Sixth Michigan troopers went with Connor's column. First Sergeant Egbert Conklin of Company B was one of them. At dawn on August 29, Connor's force surprised an unsuspecting village of Arapahos, led by Black Bear, camped on Tongue River. Many Indians were killed or taken prisoner, the camp destroyed, and their pony herd confiscated. First Sergeant Conklin was placed in charge of the captured horses. Connor then moved on, looking for villages of Sioux and Cheyenne known to be in the vicinity.[19]

On August 31, while scouting ahead of the train as it approached the Tongue River, Captain Cole and Lieutenant Moon had just reached the crest of a low ridge when they were surprised by Indians. Arapaho warriors who had survived Connor's attack two days earlier were seeking revenge. Cole was shot from his saddle and Moon barely escaped to warn the train. Returning to the scene in force, they found Cole's body pierced by five arrows as well as several bullet wounds. Troopers put Cole in a wagon, hoping to give him a proper burial later. After crossing the river next day, the train was besieged. Desperate Indians hoped to use Sawyers' isolated wagons to bargain for the return of their people and horses. A few Indians were allowed into the circle of wagons to talk and trade. It was agreed to send three Indians and three soldiers to Connor and arrange for the exchange of hostages. Two of the soldiers were Quartermaster Sergeant William Hall of Company L, and Private Henry Evans of Company F. The third man was not identified. All six left together on September 2.[20]

The three Indians returned two days later, without the soldiers, which worried Sawyers and Lovell. Captain Kellogg and his mail detail appeared the following day, having also been attacked by Indians while returning to the fort. Kellogg reported they had met the six man delegation on its way to Connor, and this is when the Indians turned around. The soldiers went on. Due to their unpredictable situation, it was decided to bury Captain Cole on the northern edge of their perimeter. On September 13, even though the Arapaho had withdrawn, Sawyers reluctantly decided to go back to Fort Connor. After going about twelve miles, the train was met by California troops, who relieved the Michigan men of their escort duties. Lovell, Kellogg, and their combined commands returned to the fort, arriving on September 16. Sergeant Hall

**MARKER ON THE SITE OF SAWYERS' FIGHT
ON THE TONGUE RIVER
ABOUT THREE MILES UP RIVER FROM CONNOR'S FIGHT**

**VIEW LOOKING EAST ALONG TONGUE RIVER -
CAPTAIN OSMER COLE WAS KILLED ON THE LOW RIDGE
ACROSS THE RIVER AT THE RIGHT OF THE PHOTO**

**SAWYERS' WAGONS WERE CIRCLED ON LOW
GROUND AT THE LEFT OF THE PHOTO -
UNMARKED GRAVES OF CAPTAIN COLE
AND TWO OTHERS ARE THERE.
TONGUE RIVER RUNS ALONG THE DISTANT TREELINE.**

and Private Evans had reached General Connor safely on the night of September 4, and they also got back to the fort.[21]

Most traveling between the forts and stations by small groups was done at night, as it was cooler and reduced the chances of encountering Indians. As an example, in early September Sergeant Wash Stewart led a four-man detail on a mail run from Deer Creek Station to Fort Connor. Starting at 8 p.m., they covered 110 miles in twenty-five hours. Captain Thomas and Private George Sharp, who were already at the fort, joined them for a more leisurely return trip, which took thirty-three hours. Stewart, who had by that time tired of the scenery, was ready to go home. So was Lieutenant Gould of Company F, who usually made the same trip in reverse, from Fort Connor to Deer Creek and back again.[22]

While Connor was chasing Indians, General Dodge came to Fort Connor on September 8 to see the progress the Sixth had made in constructing it. Dodge was very happy with the post and complimented Colonel Kidd and his regiment for their good work. On September 10, Dodge departed for Fort Laramie.[23]

Orders finally arrived in mid-September for the regiment to prepare to be relieved of duty. The day after Lovell and Kellogg returned to Fort Connor, Colonel Kidd led the Sixth out and started for Fort Laramie. In the afternoon of September 19, Colonel Kidd, Captains Kellogg and Rockafellow, and twenty men left the column for Deer Creek, arriving the next day. Captain (Acting Major) Lovell led the rest of the column on to Laramie. On the 21st, Kidd and his detachment proceeded to Fort Laramie and arrived on September 24. Two days later, Lovell and his column reached the post. There they waited until the stations were relieved by troops of the Sixteenth Kansas Cavalry.

During the time the Sixth was preparing to return east, commanders came up with a way to legally keep some of the desperately needed troops in the west. Original members of the regiment, as well as the entire brigade, would be sent back to Fort Leavenworth for discharge. Officers with key positions, or those who volunteered, would remain with the recruits from 1864 and 1865, and be transferred to the new First Michigan Veteran Cavalry to be stationed at Camp Douglas near Salt Lake City, Utah. First Lieutenant Elliott Norton, regimental Adjutant, was nursing a broken hand when he telegraphed an appeal for release from service. Norton's request was denied. The newer men were not happy with the situation either, but most accepted it without trouble. On September 27, Captain Rockafellow left Fort Laramie for Platte Bridge Station, where he took temporary command of the stations until the Sixteenth Kansas arrived. Michigan troops finally left Platte Bridge on October 18 and reached Fort Bridger on November 3. On November 17, twenty-eight men from Company B, Sixth Michigan were officially transferred to Company D, First Michigan, commanded by Captain Rockafellow. Two days later they marched for Camp Douglas.[24]

After gathering at Fort Laramie, the veterans of the Sixth Michigan Cavalry began their journey back to "the states," and Fort Leavenworth. Except for the weather, they had little trouble on their march along the Platte River, until they stopped at Fort Kearney. Indian attacks had increased along the roads, and the post commander ordered a hundred men from the Sixth to return west. Colonel Kidd and his command group had already pushed on to Fort Leavenworth, and he couldn't help his troops. Captain Thomas, leading a contingent including companies B and H, refused the order. He and Captain Kellogg were promptly arrested and confined. Captain (Acting Major) Lovell, following with another contingent, also refused the order, but was not arrested. An officer of the garrison suggested that troops and a battery of artillery be sent to force the Michigan men to comply. Lovell calmly replied that if such a thing occurred, those guns would end up at Fort Leavenworth as trophies of the Sixth Michigan Cavalry. The two contingents went on without Thomas and Kellogg, but they were soon released to continue their journey. Lovell and his troops arrived at Fort Leavenworth on November 7.[25]

Kidd and his staff were mustered out of federal service the same day, but remained in camp near the fort until all the men had returned and were released. Twenty-four veterans in Company B, a majority of them Corporals and Sergeants, were discharged on November 24. Most of the men arrived in Jackson, Michigan on November 29 or 30, where they were paid and officially released from state service. Weary warriors, who survived all the violent carnage and insanity of war, and service in the far wilderness of the west, finally went home for Christmas.[26]

At Camp Douglas, men of the First Michigan Veteran Cavalry served for nearly four more months. Of the twenty-eight men who came from Company B of the Sixth, nineteen of the men were discharged on March 10, 1866, three in February, three on April 14, two the previous December, and one in May. Those released at Salt Lake City were forced to spend their final pay for transportation home. Governor Crapo made a ten-point complaint to the War Department about the Michigan Brigade's forced, unlawful service in the west, and requested the men who had to pay their way home from Utah be reimbursed. When this was denied by the War Department, Michigan's Senators and Congressmen proposed a resolution to pay the men, and got it passed.[27]

The Sixth Michigan Cavalry made a storied contribution to this nation's military history during and after the

Civil War, and Company B contributed much to the Sixth. One of the regiment's Majors was Charles Storrs, an original member who helped recruit many of the men. The regiment's Adjutant (Elliott Norton), Sergeant-Major (William Keyes), and Commissary Sergeant (Perley Johnson) all came from Company B. One officer assigned to the company (Tom Custer) won two Medals-of-Honor. In its first engagement with the enemy, the security of the entire regiment was entrusted to Company B and its commander (Peter Weber).

A total of one hundred and sixty-three men served in Company B. Of those, fifteen were killed in action, including two officers. Twenty-two suffered wounds, and four died of them. Twenty-two were taken prisoner, at least six of whom died in captivity. Nine died of disease. Twenty-seven men were either transferred to the Invalid/Veteran Reserve Corps, or discharged due to wounds, chronic illness, or disability. Fourteen were transferred to other companies, not counting the consolidation in November 1865. One officer resigned, and one man was discharged to accept a commission in another regiment. Three men were dishonorably discharged or dismissed from service. Two men were listed as deserters, but that number was actually higher. Due to an act of Congress in 1884, which forgave desertion charges brought during the war, most records were changed to reflect an early discharge. Many men were counted in more than one category.[28]

Company B ceased to exist, but the men who survived carried the memories of the men who didn't. They held a quiet pride in having helped preserve the United States as they knew it, in spite of, but not forgetting how badly or brutally they had sometimes been treated. Some came home to Michigan and stayed. Others moved on. Most of them were good, productive citizens. All of them were human – subject to the same strengths, weaknesses, and problems people struggle with today. Each of them changed – viewing the world, and their place in it, with a new understanding.

NOTES

1   *Grand Rapids Daily Eagle,* June 19, 1865, 2 (Greeley's letter)

2   ibid; OR, Series I, Vol. 48, Pt. 2, 735 (Special Order # 65).

3   *Grand Rapids Daily Eagle,* June 19, 1865 (Greeley's letter); Haven, Appendix, 1 (Allen Pease to his Mother, June 4, 1865).

4   OR, 735-736 (Orders); James H. Kidd to his Father, July 21, 1865, Correspondence and Notebook of James H. Kidd, Bentley Historical Library, University of Michigan, Ann Arbor. Hereafter cited as Kidd's Papers.

5   OR, 975 (Stagg's report); Leroy R. Hafen and Ann W. Hafen, ed., *Diary of Captain B.F. Rockafellow – Sixth Michigan Cavalry, Powder River Campaigns and Sawyers Expedition of 1865,* Volume 12 of *Far West and the Rockies Historical Series 1820-1875,* (Glendale, California: The Arthur H. Clark Company, 1961), 153-154.

6   RSMV-36

7   ibid, 14, 21, 61, 78, 95, 136, 138, 145, 147; Haven, Appendix, 3 (Allen Pease to his wife Ella, June 27, 1865); Kidd, Notebook entry for June 24, 1865.

8   Hafen and Hafen, 158-162 (Rockafellow diary).

9   Kidd's Papers, Orders from Stagg to Kidd dated July 11, 1865; OR, 1059 (Connor to Dodge); Hafen and Hafen, 162-167 (Rockafellow diary).

10   OR, 1122-1123 (Connor to Dodge)

11   *Grand Rapids Daily Eagle,* August 18, 1865, 1 (Letter from Uknohoo).

12   George E. Hyde, *Life of George Bent, Written from his letters,* (Norman, University of Oklahoma Press, 1968) 137-222; OR, Vol. 48, Pt. 1, 23-24 (Moonlight to Curtis)

13 Hafen and Hafen, 168 (Rockafellow).

14 RSMV-36, 47, 78, 88, 128.

15 Hafen and Hafen, 168-171 (Rockafellow); Henry W. Stewart to his father, August 19, 1865, Regional History Collections, File A-284, East Bldg., East Campus, Western Michigan University, Kalamazoo.

16 Henry Stewart to his Father, August 19, 1865; *Grand Rapids Daily Eagle*, October 11, 1865, 1 (Letter from Perley Johnson to his sister); Haven, Appendix, 3-4 (Allen Pease to his mother, August 8, 1865).

17 Hafen and Hafen, 171-182 (Rockafellow); *Grand Rapids Daily Eagle*, September 18, 1865, 2 (Letter from Uknohoo dated August 22, 1865); Hyde, *Life of George Bent*, 226-228.

18 Hafen and Hafen, 186-187, (Rockafellow), 258-259 (Sawyers' report); Kidd's Papers, Letter to his Father, September 9, 1865, and notebook entry for 28 August 1865.

19 Hafen and Hafen, 192-193 (Rockafellow); Henry Stewart to his Father, September 21, 1865.

20 Hafen and Hafen, 260-262 (Sawyers); 6th Michigan Cavalry Service Records, Record group 59-14-A, Series 2, Box 122, File 7, State Archives of Michigan, Lansing.

21 Hafen and Hafen, 262-264 (Sawyers), 192-196 (Rockafellow).

22 Henry Stewart to his Father, 21 September 1865; Hafen and Hafen, 184, 188 (Rockafellow).

23 Hafen and Hafen, 190-191 (Rockafellow). Fort Connor was later renamed Fort Reno, and would be one of three forts along the Bozeman trail to be abandoned by the U.S. Army following Red Cloud's War and the treaty of 1868. The forts were burned by the Indians.

24 Henry Stewart to his Father, September 21, 1865; Hafen and Hafen, 193-202 (Rockafellow); RSMV-36.

25 Henry Stewart to his father, November 15, 1865; Haven, Appendix 8 (Allen Pease to his Mother, November 9, 1865).

26   Kidd, correspondence, November 1865; *Grand Rapids Daily Eagle,* December 2, 1865, 1; RSMV-36, Ackley, Bentley, E. Brown, Caywood, O. Clark, Conklin, Cronkright, Felton, J. Fuller, Gay, J. Johnson, McCollister, McVean, Marsac, Merrill, Wm. Moss, Newton, A. Norton, Pease, Robinson, Sharp, H.W. Stewart, N. Thomas, E. Whitney.

27   RSMV-36; Robertson, 612-613,

28   Data compiled from RSMV-36, Service Records in the National Archives, 6th Cavalry regimental records in the State Archives of Michigan, Grand Rapids Daily Eagle Articles, and the author's private collections.

AFTER THE WAR

Veteran cavalrymen returned home and became civilians again. They had lived rough for three years, and had experiences beyond the comprehension of family and friends at home. Having seen a substantial portion of the country, some wanted to see more of it. Others sought to continue the lives they led prior to the war.

First to return were men who had been in hospitals or Confederate prison camps. William Tuffs, captured in the Shenandoah Valley near the end of July, 1864, was paroled in March due to suffering from chronic diarrhea and typhoid fever, was sent to Camp Chase, Ohio. From there he was sent home on furlough. He died there on May 22, leaving a wife and two children.[1]

Harvey Smith, taken at Trevilian Station in June 1864, was released from prison in February and sent to Camp Chase. He was furloughed in March and went home. One of the first things he did was visit the widow of Stephen Stowe, and told her how and where her husband died. On a happier note, he married his sweetheart, Mary Hall, on April 25 in Grandville. Harvey reported in at Detroit when his extended leave was up, and was discharged in June. He took up farming in Jamestown Township in Ottawa County, and he and Mary lived out their lives there. Harvey Smith died in October 1920, and was buried in Grandville Cemetery. Mary died seven years later and was placed beside her husband. Their gravestones contain the words "Father" and "Mother," but they had no children of their own.[2]

William Whitney was permanently detailed to duty with the Veteran Reserve Corps in Washington in early 1864. He was discharged there on October 11, 1865, and made it home about a month before his brother Edwin. Just after the war William worked as a sawyer in Wayland and later at Sand Lake in northern Kent County. He and his wife Lovina had three daughters. William was always frail, but he outlived Lovina, who died in 1896, and a second wife who died in 1916. His family put him in the Michigan Soldiers home in Grand Rapids, where he could receive the constant care he required. William died in January 1921, and rests in the Veterans Cemetery there. Buried nearby is the detested Commissary Sergeant, Pliny Smith[3]

Daniel Stewart went home to his farm in Wyoming Township, where he stayed until he died in February 1874. He was buried in Grandville Cemetery.[4]

Oscar Stout returned to his beloved Elizabeth, and life as a farmer. He didn't travel far from home very often. One rare exception was the 50th Anniversary celebration of the Battle of Gettysburg. Oscar and Elizabeth had three children, and twenty-six more years together. Elizabeth died in October 1891. Oscar remarried in January 1907, at the age of sixty-three. On November 24, 1928, he died at his home in Cedar Springs, and was buried next to Elizabeth in Courtland Township.[5]

After deserting the column at Marysville, Kansas, Henry Welch apparently returned to Michigan and worked as a farm laborer. There is no record of his being married or having children, and he seems to have avoided officials and record keepers all his life. He died in Grand Rapids, at the home of a niece, in March 1929, and was buried in Blain Cemetery in Gaines Township, Kent County.[6]

Charges of desertion, and other offenses, blotted the records of many men in the Sixth Michigan, including those of Company B. In the 1880s, after time had softened feelings and attitudes, the War Department and Congress, full of former soldiers from both sides, acted to forgive infractions remaining on veteran's records. Over the next twenty-five years, charges were dropped or removed from the records of Oscar Stout, Henry Welch, Nathan Aldrich, Joshua Beaman, James Jones, William McGee, and William Walter.[7]

For Daniel Powers, there was no such forgiveness. In the Spring of 1865, Powers returned to Grand Rapids and established his home, knowing rumors of his disgrace would circulate for years. In July of that year, he married Mary Bennett. Daniel worked as a bookkeeper for a while, and then expanded his activities in the mercantile business. He and Mary had one daughter. Early in 1899, Daniel petitioned the Secretary of War, Russell Alger, former Lieutenant Colonel of the Sixth Michigan and Commander of the Fifth at Trevilian Station, for an honorable discharge. The petition included statements from Nelson Thomas, John Hertz, Charles Underhill, Manning Birge, and officers who had shared imprisonment with Powers. Despite the overwhelming support of other former soldiers and officers who were present at the battle, and a resolution passed by the Sixth Michigan Cavalry Association, his request was ignored, and his record remained unchanged. He applied for and received a pension, but he could not remove the stigma of his dismissal. Daniel died in April 1924 as a respected citizen and community leader, and was buried in the family plot with Mary in Oakhill Cemetery in Grand Rapids.[8]

Nelson Thomas, the last commander of Company B, returned to his home in Brighton, Livingston County. In

October 1867, he married Emma Birge, sister of his friend Manning Birge, former Major of the Sixth Michigan. Birge had originally enlisted Thomas for the Fifth Michigan in August 1862. Together, Nelson and Emma had five children, three of whom died in infancy. Emma died in 1885 of typhoid fever. In November 1887, Nelson remarried to a twenty-two-year-old, Emma Pierce Sutherland. He worked for short periods as a lumberman and farmer, but later served as a machinist for the Railroad Mail Service for nearly thirty years. Nelson Thomas died in Detroit on February 20, 1926.[9]

Not long after the war ended, the Grand Army of the Republic, or G.A.R., was organized. Posts sprang up in nearly every community across the North. In the South, the United Confederate Veterans was formed. Regimental organizations also appeared, and reunions were held. Officers of the Sixth Michigan Cavalry met every year, but the entire regiment held its first big reunion at Luce's Hall in Grand Rapids on October 20, 1875. Officers for the reunion from Company B were treasurer Solon Baxter, and Executive Committee members Perley Johnson and Charles Underhill. James Johnson was Company B's representative to the committee. Another large reunion was held in 1888, and again at Ionia on New Year's Day 1889, attended by Elliott Norton and Edmund Dikeman. Dikeman, the man who could not hold on to Sergeant's stripes, had been elected Mayor of Grand Rapids, completing his last term in 1887.[10]

Adjutant Elliott Norton returned home later than most of the men he started with in Company B. He served in the First Michigan until mustered out in March 1866. Two years later he married Lucy Bennett in Alamo Township, Kalamazoo County. Elliott and Lucy had eight children between 1869 and 1891. They moved the family to Grand Rapids, where Elliott found work that suited his administrative talents. Sometime in the 1890s, the Norton family relocated to a more rural home in North Shade Township in Gratiot County. There, in January 1899, Elliott died of the effects of a stroke he suffered six months earlier. He was buried in the family plot in Liberty Street Cemetery in Alamo Township. The cemetery is off the beaten path, seemingly neglected and forgotten, waiting for someone to remember.[11]

Solon Baxter arrived back home to Grand Rapids just after his twenty-first birthday. In March 1870 he married Kate Amelia Louise McMahon at Jackson, where he was working as a machinist. They came back to Grand Rapids, where they had five children, three of whom survived to adulthood. Solon later became a fireman. He died at the Michigan Soldiers Home on May 15, 1909 and was buried in Oakhill Cemetery.[12]

Allen Pease also came back to Grand Rapids and settled down with his wife Ella and daughter Mettie. Allen worked as a machinist, the trade he hoped to work in when he was still in the army. They had seven more children between 1866 and 1884. He died on September 19, 1922 and was buried in Oakhill Cemetery.[13]

Quartermaster Sergeant David McVean returned to farming in Bowne Township, Kent County. In November 1866 he married Eunice Parker. Eunice and David had three children, named for his parents and brother. In the 1870s David moved his family North to Kalkaska where he ran a grocery store. They moved back and forth, but were living in Kalkaska when David died in Grand Rapids on April 28, 1901. He was buried in the family plot in Fulton Street Cemetery. David has two headstones. One was put up by his family, and the other is a veteran's marker.[14]

Edwin E. Whitney joined his brother William in Wayland in December 1865. Sometime prior to 1870, Edwin married Harriet Button, nicknamed Hattie. They had one son, named

ALLEN PEASE

A post-war photo courtesy of
Eloise Haven

Harry. Edwin farmed in Wayland for a few years, and then
moved to Plainwell where he operated his own hotel. He died
there on October 22, 1898, and is buried in Hillside Cemetery.[15]

Henry Washington Stewart joined his father Daniel
on the farm in Wyoming. In March 1868, Wash married
Adeline Holden. After Daniel died in 1874, Wash moved
his family North to Antrim County. He served as Helena
Township Clerk and Supervisor before being elected County
Sheriff in 1882 and moving to Bellaire. Wash and Addie had

seven children. Addie died a year after Wash took office as Sheriff. She was buried in Helena Cemetery, just outside Alden. Wash commanded the G.A.R. post at Bellaire, which was named for Major Peter A. Weber. In 1888 Wash married Emma Barker and they had two more children. In the first decade of the new century, the Stewarts moved to Albion in eastern Calhoun County where Emma had been raised. Wash died on February 14, 1913 in Bradenton, Florida, where he apparently spent winters. His body was brought back to Michigan and he was buried next to Addie in Helena Cemetery. Physically, Henry Washington Stewart was a small man, but his courage and character were bigger than those of most other men. He was an exceptional citizen, and the epitome of a cavalryman.[16]

Walter Waite was severely injured by a falling tree, cut by a compatriot, in the Shenandoah Valley in November 1864. Discharged from Harper Hospital in Detroit in July 1865, he went home to Blendon Township in Ottawa County. In November 1873, he married Junia Payne. Charles Storrs presided over the civil ceremony. The Waite family later moved north to Scottville in Mason County, where they raised five daughters. Walter died on July 5, 1905 in Eden Township, and was buried in Lakeside Cemetery.[17]

James Kidd was a student at the University of Michigan before he went to war. He returned home to Ionia as commander of his regiment, and a Brevet Brigadier General of Volunteers. Kidd worked in his father's manufacturing business for a time, then was appointed registrar in the county land office. He married Florence McConnell in December 1871. In 1879, he became Editor and Publisher of the Ionia Sentinal. Kidd was appointed Postmaster in 1890, and spent the years 1897-1900 in Detroit when he was made Secretary of Deep

Waterways. During the post-war years, he remained a member of the Michigan National Guard. James Kidd died in Ionia on March 19, 1913, at the age of seventy-three.[18]

JAMES H. KIDD
POST WAR PHOTO - WEARING HIS "CUSTER" MEDAL

Photo Courtesy of the State Archives of Michigan

In the summer of 1913, the fiftieth anniversary of the battle of Gettysburg was celebrated. Union and Confederate veterans of the battle gathered to remember their deeds of a half-century ago, and honor their fallen comrades. The State of Michigan provided transportation for those old warriors who desired to participate. Eight men from Company B were eligible. Philip Cunningham, Frank Gross, James Merrill, Louis Marsac, Charles Storrs, Oscar Stout, Nelson Thomas, and William Whitney took part. The veteran's encampment drew the nation's attention that summer, and generated many news stories.[19]

Some men left Michigan after they were mustered out. Henry McCollister joined his brother Charles in Kansas. He became a First Lieutenant in Company B of the Nineteenth Kansas Volunteer Cavalry in October 1868, and served to April 1869. That winter the Nineteenth Kansas supported operations of the Seventh U.S. Cavalry led by Lieutenant Colonel George A. Custer. Henry married Francis Culver on July 13, 1869 at Atchison, and they made their home next to Charles and his family in Manhattan, near Fort Riley. In the 1870s Henry and Francis moved to northern California, where he clerked in a store. They moved to San Diego in southern California for a while before returning north to San Jose, where Henry was a desk clerk at Hotel Vendome. By the turn of the century, Henry was operating his own hotel in Oakland. He died there on March 11, 1909.[20]

At war's end, Lieutenant Tom Custer decided for a career in the army. He was commissioned as a Second Lieutenant in the First U.S. Infantry in February 1866, then a First Lieutenant in the Seventh U.S. Cavalry in July of the same year. That December he became the regimental Quartermaster. Tom was promoted to Captain late in 1875 and commanded Company C. He died with his brother on a hill above the Little Big Horn River on June 25, 1876.[21]

Captain Benjamin Rockafellow mustered out of service in Utah and went to Colorado and joined his father, who had moved there in 1860. Ben settled in Fremont County, west of

Colorado Springs. He worked in a mine for a season, and then turned to farming and business. Ben became Postmaster of Canon City, serving for ten years. Later he served as a state legislator. As a hobby, he wrote. While in the army he submitted articles to the Detroit Advertiser and Tribune under the pen-name "Lyons," which was his home town in Michigan. He later wrote a history of Fremont County. Ben died on March 29, 1926, and is buried in Greenwood Cemetery at Canon City.[22]

After the war, former Congressman Francis Kellogg was appointed Internal Revenue Collector for the state of Alabama. Kellogg became a carpetbagger to a degree, yet he followed a course he believed to be right. In 1868 he was elected to Congress from Alabama, but was not allowed to serve because Alabama had not yet been reconstructed and readmitted to the union. Kellogg then retired to private life, residing primarily in Ohio, but spending short periods of time in other places in the northeastern part of the country. Francis W. Kellogg died in Alliance, Ohio in January 1879. His body was brought to Grand Rapids and buried in Fulton Street Cemetery, just a few steps from the grave of Peter Weber. A section of Kent County, and a high school in that section, was named Kelloggsville to honor his service to the state and the nation.[23]

NOTES

1   Compiled Military Service Record for William J. Tuffs, Co. B, 6th Michigan Cavalry, Records of the Adjutant General's Office, Record Group 94, National Archives, Washington, D.C. Hereafter cited as Military Records.

2   Pension Application Files for Harvey and Mary Smith, SC-80482, WC-905486, Records of the Veterans Administration, Record Group 15, National Archives, Washington, D.C. Hereafter cited as Pension File(s); Headstone Inscriptions for

Harvey and Mary Smith, Grandville Cemetery, Grandville, Mi. Author's Visit – summer 2000.

3   Military Record for William B. Whitney; Pension File for William B. Whitney, SC-896801; 1870 U.S. Census, Allegan County, Michigan, Wayland, p418, National Archives Microfilm M-593, Roll 660; 1880 U.S. Census, Kent County, Michigan, Sand Lake, p418, National Archives Microfilm T-9, Roll 587; Headstone Inscriptions for William B. Whitney and Pliny Smith, Author's Visit, summer 2001.

4   1870 U.S. Census, Kent County, Michigan, Wyoming, p651, National Archives Microfilm M-593, Roll 682; Headstone Inscription for Daniel Stewart, Grandville Cemetery, Grandville, Mi. Author's Visit – summer 2000.

5   Pension File for Oscar Stout, SC-221583; Headstone Inscriptions for Oscar and Elizabeth Stout, Courtland Twp. Cemetery, Kent County, Mi. Author's Visit – summer 2000.

6   *Grand Rapids Press,* Obituary for Henry L. Welch, March 14, 1929, 28; Headstone Inscription for Henry L. Welch, Blain Cemetery, Gaines Twp., Kent County, Mi. Author's Visit – summer 2000.

7   Records of the 6th Michigan Cavalry, State Archives of Michigan, Lansing.

8   Documents for Petition requesting Honorable Service Certificate for Daniel H. Powers, Diary and Correspondence in possession of David Van Dyke, Nappanee, Indiana.; *Grand Rapids Herald,* Obituary for Daniel H. Powers, April 12, 1924, 3; Headstone Inscriptions for Daniel and Mary Powers, Oak Hill Cemetery, Grand Rapids, Mi. Author's Visit – summer 2000.

9   Pension files for Nelson and Emma Thomas, SC-123101, WC-972419,

10   Records of the G.A.R. in Michigan, State Archives of Michigan, Lansing; *Grand Rapids Eagle,* October 20, 1875, 1 (Civil War Newspaper Articles collected by Carl Bajema), Regional History Collections, Grand Rapids Public Library, Grand Rapids, Mi.; *Grand Rapids Daily Democrat,* December 13, 1888, 2 (Bajema Collection).

11   RSMV-36, 102; Pension Files for Elliott M. and Lucy L. Norton, SC-545310, WC-680559; Headstone Inscription for Elliott M. Norton, Liberty Street Cemetery, Author's Visit – Spring 2001.

12   Pension Files for Solon and Kate Baxter, SC-946294, WC-809593.

13   Haven, Epilogue.

14   Marriage Record of David E. McVean and Eunice Parker, Vol. 5, 64, County Clerk's Office, Kent County Bldg., Grand Rapids, Mi.; 1870 U.S. Census, Kent County, Michigan, Bowne Township, p79, National Archives Microfilm M-432, Roll 353; 1880 U.S. Census, Kalkaska County, Michigan, Kalkaska Village, p383, National Archives Microfilm T-9, Roll 587; 1900 U.S. Census, Kent County, Michigan, Grand Rapids, Ward 3, p318A, National Archives Microfilm T-623, Roll 721; Civil War Veteran's Obituaries, Regional History Collections, Grand Rapids Public Library, Grand Rapids, Mi.; Death Certificate, Michigan Dept. of State, Division of Vital Statistics; Headstone Inscription for David E. McVean, Fulton Street Cemetery, Author's Visit – Summer 2001.

15   1870 U.S. Census, Allegan County, Michigan, Wayland, p416R, National Archives Microfilm M-593, Roll 660; 1880 U.S. Census, Allegan County, Michigan, Plainwell Village, p421, National Archives Microfilm T-9, Roll 569; Death Certificates for Edwin E. Whitney and Harriet L. Whitney, Mich. Dept. of State, Div. of Vital Statistics; Headstone Inscriptions for Edwin E. and Harriet Whitney, Hillside Cemetery, Plainwell, Mi. Author's Visit – summer 2001.

16   Kent County Marriage records, Vol. 6, p15; 1870 U.S. Census, Kent County, Michigan, Wyoming, p651, National Archives Microfilm M-593, Roll 682; 1880 U.S. Census, Antrim County, Michigan, Helena, p6, National Archives Microfilm T-9, Roll 570; 1900 U.S. Census, Antrim County, Michigan, Helena Twp., p63A, National Archives Microfilm T-623, Roll 699; 1910 U.S. Census, Calhoun County, Michigan, Albion City, Ward 2, p30, National Archives Microfilm T-624, Roll 639; Headstone Inscription, Helena Cemetery, Alden, Mi.   Author's Visit – summer 2000.

17   Pension Files for Walter W. and Junia S. Waite, SC-126942, XC-2677-031; Death Certificate for Walter W. Waite, Mich. Dept. of State, Div. of Vital Statistics.

18   RSMV-36, 81; Kidd's Papers.

19   Grand Rapids Evening Press, 20 June 1913, 8 (Bajema Collection).

20   Pension Files for Henry H. and Francis M. McCollister, SC-538774, WC-679826; 1870 U.S. Census, Riley County, Kansas, Manhattan City, p535, National Archives Microfilm M-593, Roll 441; 1880 U.S. Census, Colusa County, California, Colusa City, p432, National Archives Microfilm T-9, Roll 64; Henry McCollister to Henry W. Stewart, 15 January 1892, Regional History Collections, File A-284, East Campus, WMU, Kalamazoo.

21   RSMV-36, 42-43.

22   Hafen and Hafen, 153; Biography of Benjamin F. Rockafellow, Fremont County, Colorado.

23   *Grand Rapids Eagle*, Obituary for Francis W. Kellogg, January 16, 1879, 1; January 17, 1879, 2.

APPENDIX A

CAMPS LEE
AND KELLOGG

On the old campus of Grand Rapids Central High School, now the campus of City High School, there is a marker identifying Camps Kellogg and Lee, and the units organized there. It stands a block away from the actual site. Both camps were enclosed by what is now Lyon Street on the south, Michigan Street on the north, Prospect Avenue on the west side, and Union Avenue on the east.

Camp Kellogg, named for Congressman Kellogg, was created first when the Sixth Michigan Cavalry moved from low ground near the Grand River to the head of Lyon Street on the ridge above town. Crude, one story barracks were built for the men, and shelters for the horses. Barracks and officer's tents were probably on a line or lines along Prospect near the corner of Lyon, with the horse shelters along Lyon Street. The shelters may have been corduroyed with logs to prevent disease of the horse's hooves. Directly in front of and on the east side of the barracks was likely the parade ground, with the area farther to the east toward Union Avenue being used for mounted drill.

Camp Lee, probably named for Colonel George W. Lee, a staff officer at Detroit, was created when the Seventh Michigan Cavalry began forming in the fall of 1862, just after the Sixth. The excess men who were recruited for the Sixth were to become the nucleus of the Seventh, as it had been with the Fifth and Sixth. The Seventh occupied the same type of barracks which probably extended north along Prospect toward Michigan, then still called Bridge Street. A Grand Rapids Daily Eagle article from the fall of 1863 described a fence which was built to help hold conscripted men at Camp Lee which extended out into Bridge Street.

As time went on, better barracks were built, and the name Camp Kellogg was rarely used. The entire military reservation became known as Camp Lee, or Lee Barracks. When the war ended, the camps were abandoned and buildings torn down. Subsequent construction removed any archaeological material which might have shed more light on Civil War camp life in Grand Rapids.[1]

**PLAQUE IDENTIFYING UNITS ORGANIZED
AT CAMPS KELLOGG AND LEE
(CAMPUS OF GRAND RAPIDS CENTRAL HIGH SCHOOL)**

Photo by the Author

NOTES

1   Asa B. Isham, *An Historical Sketch of the Seventh Regiment Michigan Volunteer Cavalry
– From its Organization, in 1862, to its Muster Out, in 1865,* (New York: Town Topics
Publishing Company, 1893) 7-12; Bajema Collection.

APPENDIX B

THE FIGHT ON JUNE 30, 1863

There are questions that are difficult to answer, and spark a certain amount of speculation after reading the official report by the regimental commander and several accounts from members of Company B concerning the fight west of Hanover on June 30, 1863.

Colonel Gray reported the regiment drove enemy skirmishers to their guns, and found they were supported by a large body of cavalry. He then decided to withdraw. Gray reported a second body of enemy cavalry attacked his flank, at which time he left Companies B & F under Weber's command to hold them back while the rest of the regiment moved on to Hanover.[1]

James Kidd stated in his book they went off the road, through a wheat field, and up on the crest of a ridge where they spotted a large force of enemy cavalry supported by artillery. The artillery opened on them, forcing them to withdraw, leaving Weber and his two companies to hold off the enemy.[2]

Daniel Powers wrote that by the second charge, which went through a patch of woods, his hat had been shot off, his horse had five holes in him, and they had covered many miles back-and-forth. At the beginning of the third charge, which was a reaction to being flanked, his horse was killed and he was taken prisoner.[3]

Daniel Stewart said when they came upon the enemy "they were to(o) strong", so "we fell back and formed in line of battle. Mean(while) the rebs had got in our rear with about three thousand cavalry…when they made a charge on us…we fired on them with carbines and revolvers…then commenced a race we retreating…our company was cut off from the rest of the regiment and drew the rebel force after us." His horse was also wounded and he said the animal carried him "about five miles before he gave out." Then he wrote, "We rallied and drove the rebs three times." He said after the third charge, they "went down to a house…but the rebs were all around us…we rode into a piece of woods and lay there 'til near sundown and saw the rebs pass by all the afternoon within forty rods." As the sun set they were spotted, and they raced out of the woods to safety as the rebels shelled the woods.[4]

Allen Pease stated in a letter, "We were surrounded by two brigades of rebel cavalry and our company cut off from the regiment. We took for the woods and about three hundred rebs after us. We turned and made a charge with our sabers on them and they turned and run. They charged on us and shot a good many of our horses. We charged on them five times and they on us four. We had 14 men and our first lieutenant taken prisoner. They wounded one man in the neck after they had taken him. We heard from them yesterday. They are in a parole camp at West Chester, Pennsylvania."[5]

Casualties for June 30 were reported from Company B as one man wounded and fifteen missing and presumed captured, compared to Company F who had one man wounded and one man captured. It is amazing that no soldier in the squadron was killed.[6]

Even with all the fascinating individual accounts from participants, it is very difficult to pinpoint where all the action took place, and which patch or patches of woods troopers from Company B fought through or hid in. Much of the area, known locally as Mount Pleasant, is generally the same as it appeared in 1863. The distances the participants said they covered during the fight are questionable. Riding miles in one direction would have taken them out of the fight altogether, or involved them in another taking place nearby. Excitement and adrenaline may have influenced their accounts. A final question is why were casualties from Company F so much less than Company B?

John Krepps discusses these subjects in Chapter Eight and Appendix I of his excellent work, "A Strong and Sudden Onslaught – The Cavalry Action at Hanover, Pennsylvania."

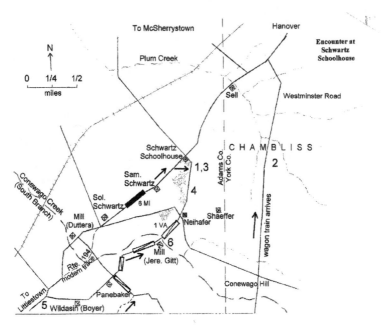

Map by David Weaver" and "Courtesy of Colecraft Industries Map provided by John T. Krepps, from his book "A Strong and Sudden Onslaught – The Cavalry Action at Hanover, Pennsylvania." First contact occurred in the area of number 4.

NOTES

1 Robertson, 584.

2 Kidd, 127.

3 Daniel H. Powers to his Parents, July 19, 1863.

4 Daniel Stewart to Margaret Murray, July 24, 1863.

5 Allen Pease to his Mother, July 18, 1863.

6 RSMV-36; Grand Rapids Daily Eagle, July 25, 1863, 1; New York Times, July 28, 1863, Cavalry Casualties from June 30 to July 20, 1863.

APPENDIX C

DANIEL POWERS AT TREVILIAN STATION

In his report after the Battle of Trevilian Station, Brigadier General Custer stated, "…the space over which we fought was so limited that there was actually no place which could be called under cover, or in other words the entire ground was in range of the enemy guns. This fact induced the officer who had assumed charge of the pack trains, caissons, headquarters wagons, and all the property we had captured, to seek without orders a place of safety. In doing so he conducted them into the lines of the enemy, where they were captured. In causing this mishap he acted on his own responsibility, impelled by fear alone, and I might add that for his conduct on this occasion the President of the United States has dismissed him from the service for cowardice and treachery." [1]

Lieutenant Harmon Smith of Company F, Seventh Michigan Cavalry stated in his account of the battle, "It was my fortune to be near General Custer, and of course in the middle of the fray. One officer was so muddled that he asked Custer if it would not be best to move certain things for safety to the rear. The General said, "Yes, by all means," and then added, "Where in hell is the rear?"[2]

Captain Daniel H. Powers, commander of Company B and the brigade trains that day, was the officer both men described.

According to Custer's report and Confederate accounts of the battle, the Michigan Brigade was heavily engaged on the west and north sides of their perimeter by elements of Hampton's Division, and receiving some fire from the east which was probably the Fifteenth Virginia Cavalry. Very little enemy fire was coming from the south. A map of Trevilian Station from Battles and Leaders of the Civil War, and another from Colonel Swank's book, show Custer's captured trains well south of the road, on the left of Fitz Lee's Division as it charged in. Items taken from Custer's headquarters wagons were in the possession of Colonel Thomas Munford and others who rode with the Second Virginia Cavalry that day. The Second Virginia was on Lee's left.[3]

After getting Custer's consent, Powers took the trains to the southeast, toward a stand of trees where he thought he could better protect the wagons. At the same time, elements of Lee's Division charged in, and the trains were overwhelmed. One company, spread out among the wagons and other vehicles could not hold off parts of two or three regiments of Confederate cavalry. Powers and four of his men were captured, and another who was seriously wounded would be left the following night. Eight others were wounded and made it back to the perimeter. More men would have been taken had the Confederate's attention not been focused on the contents of the wagons.

Did Captain Powers act out of cowardice and treachery as claimed by Custer? No.

Could Captain Powers have been as confused and disoriented as many others in the brigade that day, including Custer? Yes.

Custer was understandably angry at losing his trains and headquarters wagons. His letters from his wife were published in Richmond newspapers. He and Libby were publicly discussed and trashed by the so-called genteel southern aristocracy. This was very painful for both of them. But blaming Powers and seeking his dismissal was wrong, and reporting that Powers "acted on his own responsibility, impelled by fear alone," was a false statement. As shown in Lieutenant Harmon Smith's account, he asked for and received Custer's permission to move the trains to what he thought was a safer and more defendable place.[4]

In 1899 Powers requested an Honorable Service Certificate from the Secretary of War of the United States, Russell A. Alger. Accompanying his request was a resolution by the Sixth Michigan Cavalry Association, and several statements. Some were from former officers from Michigan regiments who had been imprisoned with Powers. Other statements were from veterans of the Sixth Michigan Cavalry. Well known and respected former enlisted men Charles Underhill and John Hertz, as well as former officers Manning Birge and Nelson Thomas, who all were present at the battle and knew what occurred, provided their support for Powers.[5]

Perhaps Powers timing may have been bad, and there was no desire to change the record. Whatever the reason or reasons were, Powers was denied an Honorable Service Certificate. The Spanish-American War had just ended and Alger had enough to do with troops deploying all over the globe. Powers also had to refute the actions of two national martyrs. Who in the government would admit that General George Armstrong Custer had made a false statement, and President Abraham Lincoln had acted in a rash and hasty manner? It was an issue nobody in the government was prepared to deal with.

So Daniel H. Powers remained a dismissed officer. If he really had been a coward, he would have moved away from western Michigan, to a place where he and his record weren't so well known. Yet he stayed, built his life and raised a family in the same place he started from. There is no record, other than Custer's report, of his ever being blamed or accosted by anyone who was present at Trevilian Station.

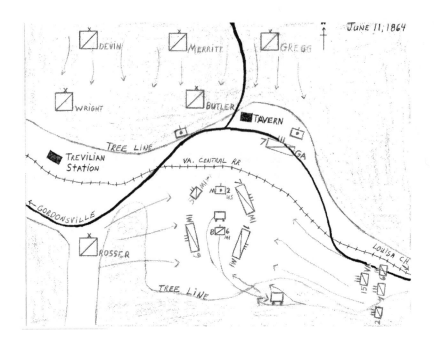

NOTES

1   OR, Series I, Vol. 36, Pt. 1, 824 (Custer's report).

2   Lee, 230 (Smith's account).

3   OR, Vol. 36, Pt.1, 823-824 (Custer); B&L, Vol. 4, 235; Swank, 17, 103.

4   Lee, 230

5   Documents in Support of Request for Honorable Service Certificate, Diary and Correspondence for Daniel Powers, in Possession of David Van Dyke, Nappanee, Indiana.

APPENDIX D

COMPANY B AND THE SIXTH MICHIGAN CAVALRY IN THE WEST

Nobody in the Sixth Michigan Cavalry wanted to go west and fight Indians, yet they went anyway...under protest. Colonel Kidd knew that if they mutinied or caused too much trouble for commanders, it would negatively mark their entire period of service, even though it had been particularly outstanding up to that time. He was able to get most of the men to understand that, and continue on in spite of their justified anger. They still managed to make a major contribution to the nation's history on the plains and along the Bozeman Trail.

The men felt they had earned the right to go home. They never intended to fight Indians in the west. Fighting the Confederates and reunifying the nation was the reason most of them enlisted. They felt western troops, who had not been in direct and prolonged opposition to the rebels, as the Michigan men had, were responsible for their own war.

On the return trip to Fort Leavenworth, when they were stopped at Fort Kearny by Nebraskan troops with the intent to send them back west, they nearly fought against fellow volunteers. Commanders of Companies B and H were arrested and confined to force them to go back. Another commander, Acting Major Don Lovell was threatened with the same treatment. It is interesting to note that they all would have willingly fought against fellow federal troops to get home rather than stay and fight Indians they had no quarrel with, and they were confident in their ability to win that fight.

Fort Connor, built by the Sixth Michigan Cavalry and later renamed Fort Reno, was an important post during the war, which was called Red Cloud's War, with the northern plains tribes of Lakota Sioux, Northern Cheyenne, and Northern Arapahoe. Abandoned after the treaty of 1868, it was one of three forts along the Bozeman Trail (Forts Phil Kearny, C.F. Smith, and Reno) burned down by the temporarily victorious Indians.

Eleven years after the Sixth went home, on the same hunting grounds the Indians desperately fought to hold, Company B would lose its former brigade commander and one of its former members in the final major Indian victory during more than three centuries of conflict.

Monument on the site of Deer Creek Station, Glenrock, Wyoming. The station was a long, single story log building, with partitioned rooms inside, and a closed, high-fenced corral in the back for the horses. It had two outbuildings for kitchen/ mess hall, and blacksmith shop.

Looking west from Deer Creek Station along the old telegraph road. The bluff at left center was featured prominently in contemporary drawings of the station.

Parade ground of old Fort Kearny, Nebraska looking southeast.

Parade ground looking east toward the guard house.

Location of the guardhouse at the northeast corner of the parade ground, where Captains Thomas and Kellogg were briefly held by Nebraska state troops.

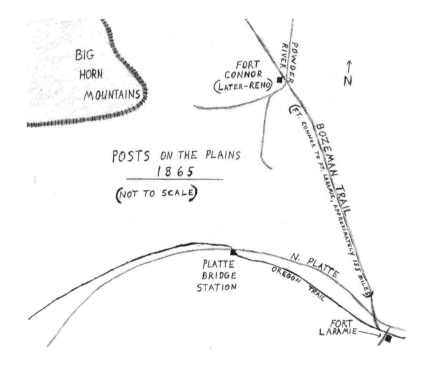

BIG
HORN
MOUNTAINS

FORT
CONNOR
(LATER-RENO)

POWDER RIVER

↑
N

(FT. CONNOR TO FT. LARAMIE, APPROXIMATELY 155 MILES)

BOZEMAN TRAIL

POSTS ON THE PLAINS
1865
(NOT TO SCALE)

N. PLATTE

PLATTE
BRIDGE
STATION

OREGON TRAIL

FORT
LARAMIE

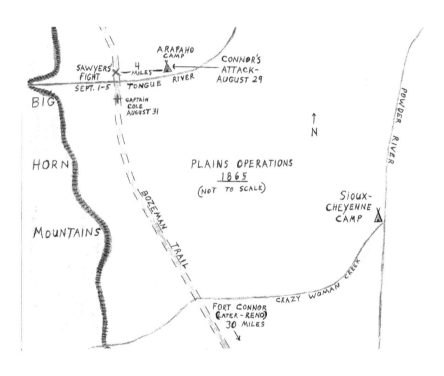

BIBLIOGRAPHY

Adjutant General's Office of Michigan. *Record of Service of Michigan Volunteers in the Civil War 1861-1865.* Vols. 3, 36, 40. Kalamazoo: Ihling Bros & Everhard, 1905.

Bajema, Carl. Civil War Newspaper Article Collection. Grand Rapids History & Special Collections, Archives, Grand Rapids Public Library.

Bush, Garry L. "The Sixth Michigan Cavalry at Falling Waters: The End of the Gettysburg Campaign." *The Gettysburg Magazine* 9 (July 1993): 109-115.

Butler, M.C. "The Cavalry Fight at Trevilian Station." *Battles and Leaders of the Civil War* 4 (1887-1888): 237-239.

Cooke, Philip St. George. *Cavalry Tactics: or Regulations for the Instruction, Formations, and Movements of the Cavalry of the Army and Volunteers of the United States.* vol 1. 1862. Reprint. Mittituck, N.Y.: J.M. Carroll & Co., 1999.

Detroit Advertiser and Tribune, 1861-1865.

Dyer, Frederick H. *A Compendium of the War of the Rebellion,* 3 vols. Des Moines, Iowa: The Dyer Publishing Company, 1908.

Franks, George. "The Final Battle of the Gettysburg Campaign: Falling Waters, Maryland 14 July 1863." *Strategy and Tactics Magazine* 246 (Oct/Nov 2007): 54-58.

Grand Rapids Daily Eagle, 1861-1865.

Gross, Frank. Diaries, 1864-1865. Bentley Historical Library, University of Michigan.

Hafen, Leroy R. and Ann W. Hafen, eds. *Powder River Campaigns and Sawyers' Expedition of 1865*. Gendale, California: Arthur H. Clark Co., 1961.

Hamilton, Richard L. *"Oh! Hast Thou Forgotten" Michigan Cavalry in the Civil War: The Gettysburg Campaign*. Tucson, Arizona, 2008.

Haven, Eloise A. ed. *In the Steps of a Wolverine: The Civil War Letters of a Michigan Cavalryman*. Kentwood, Michigan 2005.

Hebard, Grace R. and E.A. Brininstool. *The Bozeman Trail. vol. 1*. Lincoln: University of Nebraska Press, 1922.

Hyde, George E. Edited by Savoie Lottinville. *Life of George Bent: Written from his Letters*. Norman: University of Oklahoma Press, 1968.

Imboden, John D. "The Confederate Retreat from Gettysburg." *Battles and Leaders of the Civil War* 3 (1887-1888): 397-406.

Isham, Asa B. *An Historical Sketch of the Seventh Regiment Michigan Volunteer Cavalry – From its Organization in 1862, to its Muster Out, in 1865*. New York: Town Topics Publishing Company, 1893.

Kidd, James H. Correspondence and Notebook. Bentley Historical Library, University of Michigan.

_____. *Personal Recollections of a Cavalryman with Custer's Michigan Cavalry Brigade in the Civil War*. 1908. Reprint. Grand Rapids, Michigan: The Black Letter Press, 1969.

Krepps, John T. *A Strong and Sudden Onslaught. The Cavalry Action at Hanover, Pennsylvania*. Orrtanna, Pennsylvania: Colecraft Industries, 2008.

Lee, William O. Comp. *Personal and Historical Sketches and Facial History of and by Members of the Seventh Regiment, Michigan Volunteer Cavalry 1862-1865*. Detroit, Michigan: 7th Michigan Cavalry Association, 1902.

BIBLIOGRAPHY

Longacre, Edward G. *The Cavalry at Gettysburg: A Tactical Study of Mounted Operations during the Civil War's Pivotal Campaign, 9 June – 14 July 1863.* Lincoln: University of Nebraska Press, 1986.

————. *Custer and his Wolverines: The Michigan Cavalry Brigade, 1861-1865.* Conshohocken, Pa.: Combined Publishing, 1997.

Lydens, Z. Z. ed. *The Story of Grand Rapids.* Grand Rapids, Mi.: Kregel Publications, 1967.

Merington, Marguerite, ed. *The Custer Story: The Life and Letters of General George A. Custer and His Wife Elizabeth.* New York: The Devin-Adair Co., 1950.

Miller, William E. "The Cavalry Battle Near Gettysburg." *Battles and Leaders of the Civil War 3* (1887-1888): 420-429.

New York Times, July 29, 1863.

Porter, Horace. "Five Forks and the Pursuit of Lee." *Battles and Leaders of the Civil War 4* (1887-1888): 709-722.

Powers, Daniel H. Correspondence and Diary in possession of David Van Dyke, Nappanee, Indiana.

Records of the Sixth Michigan Volunteer Cavalry Regiment. State Archives of Michigan.

Robertson, John. Comp. *Michigan in the War.* Lansing, Michigan: W.S. George & Co., 1882.

Rodenbough, Theo. F. "Sheridan's Richmond Raid." *Battles and Leaders of the Civil War 4* (1887-1888): 188-193.

————. "Sheridan's Trevilian Raid." *Battles and Leaders of the Civil War 4* (1887-1888): 233-236.

Stewart, Daniel. Correspondence. Regional History Collections, East Bldg., East Campus, Western Michigan University.

Stewart, Henry Washington. Correspondence. Regional History Collections, East Bldg., East Campus, Western Michigan University.

Swank, Walbrook D. *Battle of Trevilian Station: The Civil War's Greatest and Bloodiest All Cavalry Battle, With Eyewitness Memoirs."* Shippensburg, Pa.: Burd Street Press, 1994.

The War of the Rebellion: A Compilation of the Official Records of the Union and Confederate Armies. 130 vols. Washington, D.C.: Government Printing Office, 1880-1901.

Urwin, Gregory J.W. *Custer Victorious: The Civil War Battles of General George Armstrong Custer.* Rutherford, N.J.: Fairleigh Dickinson University Press, 1983.

_____. *The United States Cavalry: An Illustrated History.* Poole, Dorset, U.K.: Blandford Press, 1983

Utley, Robert M. *Frontiersmen in Blue – The United States Army and the Indian 1848-1865.* Lincoln: University of Nebraska Press, 1967.

Wittenburg, Eric J. *Glory Enough For All – Sheridan's Second Raid and the Battle of Trevilian Station.* Washington, D.C.: Brassey's 2001.

_____. *One Continuous Fight – The Retreat from Gettysburg and the Pursuit of Lee's Army of Northern Virginia, July 4-14, 1863.* New York and California: Savas Beatie, 2008, 2011.

Index of Persons

Ackley, Newton, 12
Aldrich, Nathan C., 107, 143
Alger, Russell A., 9, 25, 40, 63, 143, 165
Archer, James, 50
Arsnoe, Augustus, 75, 94
Arsnoe, James, 75, 94
Averill, Latham, 36

Bacon (Custer), Elizabeth (Libby), 11, 95, 106, 164
Baker, Asa, 76, 107
Barker (Stewart), Emma, 147
Batson, Charles, 12, 54
Baxter, Solon W., 12, 54, 121, 144, 145
Beaman, Joshua R., 76, 107, 143
Benham (Stout), Elizabeth Ann, 10, 62, 121, 142
Bennett (Norton), Lucy, 144
Bennett (Powers), Mary, 143
Bentley, Solon M., 12, 25, 35, 79, 116
Birge, Manning, 91, 144, 165
Birge (Thomas), Emma, 144
Blair, Austin, 1, 7, 8, 10, 23, 25
Black Bear, 130
Black Kettle, 124
Blood, Abel, 75, 120
Bloomburg, Charles W., 107
Bodley, Thomas, 76
Bolza, Charles E., 2, 23, 54, 63, 64, 65
Bowman, Lewis, 12, 25, 57

Boyer, Mitch, 127
Bridger, Jim, 127
Brockenbrough, John, 50, 52
Brown, Eliza, 92
Brown, Ezra, 12, 35, 79, 107
Brown, Simeon, 8
Buford, John, 47
Burder, John, 76, 104
Button (Whitney), Harriet, 145

Campbell, Archibald, 12, 54
Caywood, David G., 12, 23, 35, 107
Chambliss, John, 36
Chiles, Buck, 90
Church, Isaac R., 12, 105
Clark, Isaac, 12, 19
Clark, Orozene R., 12
Clay, Henry, 12, 23
Cole, Garrett, 12, 23
Cole, Osmer, 129-132
Collins, Caspar, 125
Colton, Alva, 12, 54
Comstock, Warren C., 2, 22
Conklin, Egbert S., 6, 71, 75, 77, 94, 130
Conkling, Andrew J., 9, 12
Connor, Patrick, 122, 123, 125-131, 133
Cook, Alexander H., 105, 106
Cooke, Philip St. George, 5, 33, 78
Copeland, Joseph, 22, 30, 31

Covell, Elliott, 63
Crapo, Henry, 117, 135
Crawford, Francis, 55
Crawford, George, 55
Creevey, William, 125, 126
Cronkright, James M., 12, 116
Culver (McCollister), Francis, 149
Cunningham, Philip, 12, 107, 149
Curry, Enoch W., 12, 20
Custer, George A., 11, 31, 37, 39-41, 45-47, 49, 52, 57, 66, 70, 71, 75, 78, 81, 83, 84, 87, 90-92, 95, 100, 102, 105, 106, 114, 149, 163-165
Custer, Thomas W., 105, 106, 116, 136, 149

Dahlgren, Ulric, 78
Deane, Charles, 102
Devin, Thomas, 108, 115
Dikeman, Edmund B., 6, 64, 66, 79, 144
Dix, John, 62
Dodge, Grenville, 119, 120, 123, 133
Dooley, Daniel, 116, 126
Doty, Henry W., 76
Durham, Peter, 116

Early, Jubal, 96, 102-104, 108
Eaton, Frank M., 107
Elmore, Byron A., 76, 89
English, Joseph M., 107
English, Martin J., 76
Evans, Alson, 116
Evans, Henry, 130, 133
Ewell, Richard, 46

Felton, Smith, 12
Fields, George E., 75
Fisher, Samuel E., 116
Flint, Lewis L., 116
Foote, Thadeus, 8, 25, 63

Fuller, Daniel, 12, 120, 121
Fuller, John D., 12, 96
Furnier, Schofield, 116

Gay, James D., 12, 35
Glazier, Calvin R., 12, 23, 121
Gooch, Horace N., 12, 54
Gorman, Thomas, 12
Goucher, Charles, 76-78
Goucher, Homer, 76, 77, 94
Gould, John, 133
Grant, U.S., 79, 83, 84, 96, 111, 114, 117
Gray, George, 7-9, 31, 32, 57, 66, 81, 159
Greeley, Stephen, 9, 10, 18, 66, 119, 120
Green, John, 12, 121
Green, Nathan, 12
Green, William, 12, 67
Greenman, Martin R., 12, 23
Gregg, David, 37, 39, 40
Griffith, Gilbert D., 12, 54
Gross, Frank, 12, 84, 96, 149

Haist, Jacob, 12
Hale, Hiram, 8
Hall, John R., 12, 23
Hall (Smith), Mary, 141, 142
Hall, William, 130, 131
Halleck, Henry, 10, 78
Hammond, Alfred, 13, 19
Hampton, Wade, 37, 40, 70, 73, 92, 93, 164
Hertz, John, 143, 165
Heth, Henry (Harry), 50
Hill, Ambrose P., 57
Hill, Daniel H., 62
Hobart, Henry, 71
Holden (Stewart), Adaline (Addie), 146, 147
Hoskins, Madison J., 75
Howe, George W., 13, 67

Imboden, John, 47

Johnson, Bushrod, 114
Johnson, James E., 6, 71, 79, 105, 107, 120, 144
Johnson, Nelson M., 13, 23
Johnson, Perley W., 13, 77, 94, 107, 136, 144
Jones, James R., 76, 121, 143
Jones, Robert R., 76, 95, 126

Keater, James, 6, 23
Kellogg, Francis W., 1, 3, 5, 7, 8, 18, 64, 129, 150, 155
Kellogg, James, 129-131, 133-135, 173
Kettle, Frederick S., 13, 96
Kettle, Matthew J., 77
Keyes, William E., 6, 34, 54, 71, 136
Kidd, James H., 2, 3, 29, 39, 50, 52, 66, 71, 78, 81, 84-86, 88, 91, 96, 100, 102, 108, 119-122, 125-128, 133-135, 147, 148, 159, 167
Kilpatrick, Judson, 31, 45-50, 52, 70, 78-80, 86
Konkle, Frank, 36

Labell, George H., 77, 120
Lee, Fitzhugh, 33, 36, 40, 70, 90-92, 101, 113, 115, 164
Lee, George W., 156
Lee, Robert E., 25, 36, 39, 47, 57, 62, 64, 70, 85, 96, 114
Lewis, James N., 13, 54
Lincoln, Abraham, 1, 19, 73, 78, 95, 96, 115, 165
Longstreet, James, 69
Lorsey, Charles, 13
Lovell, Don G., 33, 57, 61, 70, 91, 129, 131, 133-135, 168
Lowe, William, 13

McBride (Whitney), Lovina, 10, 142

McCall, Donald T., 76
McCollister, Charles, 149
McCollister, Henry H., 13, 54, 149
McCollum, George H., 75, 78, 126
McConnell (Kidd), Florence, 147
McGee, William J., 107, 143
McGowen, Thomas, 13 35
McIntosh, John, 39, 41
McLarren, Andrew J., 76, 95
McMahon (Baxter), Kate A.L., 145
McVean, David E., 6, 35, 71, 74, 107, 145
Mann, William, 7, 8, 22
Marsac, Lewis, 13, 54, 149
Martin, Alonzo R., 13, 54
Maxfield, John A., 6, 23
Mayfield, Oakland W., 13, 54
Mead, Charles, 78
Mead, Ezra, 107
Meade, George G., 31, 62, 69, 70, 73, 79, 84, 115
Merrill, James H., 13, 149
Merritt, Wesley, 100, 102, 108, 111, 114
Milton, John, 75, 121
Mitchell, William H., 13
Molloy, John C., 13, 23, 126
Monroe, William, 13, 67
Moon, Robert, 129, 130
Moore, Richard, 76, 107
Mosby, John, 25, 58, 105, 108
Moss, George F., 75, 77
Moss, William, 13, 77
Munford, Thomas, 164
Munson, David, 13

Neal, Flavious J., 13, 54
Neal, James R., 13, 102
Newton, John, 13, 35, 71, 88, 107
North, Frank, 127, 128
Norton, Augustus, 13
Norton, Elliott M., 11, 13, 19, 23, 55, 61, 99, 134, 136, 144, 145

Odell, Orson B., 6, 67
Onweller, William, 76, 94

Parker, Charles A., 75-77, 79, 105
Parker (McVean), Eunice, 145
Patten, Charles, 6, 65, 66
Patten, George T., 6, 10, 23, 24, 54-56, 65, 71
Patten, Lydia, 24
Patten, Lyman E., 8, 65, 66
Patten, Lyman W., 65
Patten, Sarah, 65
Payne (Waite), Junia, 147
Pease, Allen D., 2, 10, 13, 19, 23, 57, 66, 121, 145, 146, 160
Pease, Emma, 145
Pease, Mettie, 145
Pelton, Francis, 13, 54
Pennington, Alexander, 37, 39, 41
Perry, Arthur E., 75
Pettigrew, James J., 50, 52
Pickett, George, 39, 50, 113, 114
Platt, John P., 6, 54
Pleasonton, Alfred, 80
Pope, John, 3, 117, 119, 120
Post, Charles S., 76, 100
Potter, Harvey B., 6, 23, 54
Powers, Daniel H., 6, 22-24, 34-36, 61, 62, 66, 69, 71, 77, 79, 92, 94, 95, 143, 159, 163-165

Randall, George R., 76,
Red Cloud, 168
Reynolds, William, 76, 95,
Richmond, Rebecca, 10
Robinson, Edwin E., 6, 23
Rockafellow, Benjamin, 120, 121, 125-127, 133, 134, 149, 150
Rogers, Remus, 13, 54,
Rossell, Abram, 13, 54
Rosser, Thomas, 83, 84, 91, 92, 102, 108

Royce, David, 52, 63
Runnels, Curtis, 13
Rust, David, 13, 67

Sanders, Joseph M., 116
Sawyers, James A., 128, 130, 131
Schofield, Edgar, 76
Seeley, Harvey, 13, 19, 94
Sharp, George, 13, 133
Shepard, S.G., 50, 51, 55
Sheridan, Philip H., 80, 84, 85, 86, 87, 90, 93, 96, 100, 104, 105, 108, 111, 113
Sherman, William T., 95, 115,
Skeels, Dorr, 6, 23
Sliter, Josiah T., 13, 54
Smith, Harmon, 92, 163, 165,
Smith, Harvey, 2, 14, 35, 66, 94, 141
Smith, Jacob, 76, 95
Smith, J.R., 11
Smith, Joseph, 116, 126
Smith, Pliny, 6, 61, 77, 142
Stagg, Peter, 108, 119-121
Stahel, Julius, 21, 31
Stanton, Edwin M., 1
Stewart, Daniel, 2, 14, 34, 121, 142, 146, 160
Stewart, Henry W., 2, 3, 14, 19, 34, 35, 54, 69, 71, 72, 107, 133, 146, 147
Stoneman, George, 75
Storrs, Charles E., 2, 22, 23, 39, 40, 136, 147, 149
Stout, Oscar, 2, 10, 14, 35, 62, 101, 107, 108, 121, 142, 143, 149
Stowe, Stephen L., 2, 10, 14, 19, 35, 71, 73, 79, 94, 141
Stuart, J.E.B., 5, 19, 31, 36, 39, 41, 46, 47, 62, 70, 71, 84, 85, 87
Sutherland (Thomas), Emma Pierce, 144
Swain, Sardius B., 76, 88
Swarthout, John H., 76, 121

Thomas, George, 105
Thomas, Nelson C., 6, 23, 46, 71,
    79, 95, 105, 107, 121, 126, 133-
    135, 143, 144, 149, 165, 173
Thomson, John C., 116
Thompson, Henry, 63
Tillapaw, Lafayette, 76
Torbert, Alfred, 81, 100, 101, 108
Trumbley, Anthony, 116
Trumbley, Benjamin, 14, 23
Tuffs, William J., 14, 35, 101, 141
Turner, Byron, 76,
Turner, James P., 76

Underhill, Charles A., 76, 143, 144,
    165

Vanetten, Jacob, 76, 120, 121
Vinton, Harvey, 91, 100, 108
Vose, Samuel R., 76

Wait, Justus, 14, 23
Waite, Walter W., 14, 35, 147

Walker, Edward N., 116
Walter, William C., 76, 143
Waters, Elijah, 8, 39
Watkins, Charles W., 14, 35, 67
Weare, Daniel, 9
Weber, Peter A., 3-5, 7, 10, 29, 32-
    34, 36, 39-41, 48-52, 54, 63, 64,
    66, 79, 147, 150, 159
Webster, James, 14, 20
Welch, Henry, 2, 14, 121, 142, 143
Whitney, Edwin E., 2, 14, 19, 23, 35,
    79, 99, 142, 145, 146
Whitney, Harry, 146
Whitney, William B., 2, 10, 14, 75,
    142, 149
Wilson, James, 80, 81
Winkworth, Robert, 76, 77
Withey, Solomon, 8, 66
Wright, Morris, 116
Wyndham, Percy, 20, 21

Yeomans, Myndert, 116

Cover Art: Falling Waters Drawing by Alfred Waud – Library of Congress
6th Michigan Battle Flag Courtesy of the Michigan Capitol Committee –
Photo by Peter Glendinning

Made in the USA
Charleston, SC
21 May 2012